I0759960

TO KNOW HIM

TO KNOW HIM

A 90-DAY INVITATION *to Come to God as You Are*

DR. HENRY CLOUD

NEW YORK NASHVILLE

Worthy
Hachette Book Group
1290 Avenue of the Americas, New York, NY 10104
worthypublishing.com
@WorthyPub

First Edition: October 2025

Additional copyright information is on page 232.

Print book interior design by Timothy Shaner, NightandDayDesign.biz

Library of Congress Control Number: 2025942566

ISBNs: 9781546009238 (paper over board), 9781546009245 (ebook)

Printed in the United States of America

LSC-C

Printing 1, 2025

A Note from the Author

Dear Fellow Sojourner,

I wanted to welcome you to this journey of getting closer to God and even helping others to do the same. In my own life, as the book explains, it certainly was a journey, with many ups and downs. For most people I know, as well as most of the characters in the Bible, that is true for them as well. Getting to know God and growing in your spiritual life is hardly ever a straight line. But at the same time, through all the twists and turns, times of strong enlightenment and other times of feeling lost, there is a sure direction. God promises that, and He fulfills that promise. The direction is always "to Him." Getting closer to Him, and knowing Him more and more intimately. The journey is worth it! My prayer for you is that this devotional will help you along the way, prompting deeper and deeper moments with Him, more small steps of faith that might feel risky, and even some big leaps. I am praying for you!

God Bless,

Henry

TO KNOW HIM

1

I Don't Know How to Tell Them

But in your hearts revere Christ as Lord. Always be prepared to give an answer to everyone who asks you to give the reason for the hope that you have. But do this with gentleness and respect, keeping a clear conscience, so that those who speak maliciously against your good behavior in Christ may be ashamed of their slander.

—1 Peter 3:15–16

Have you ever struggled to share something important with someone you care about?

Me too.

Since I was about ten years old, I have had an issue . . . and although it is better, it is still unresolved in my heart with so many of you . . . my friends. I won't name you by name here, but maybe you will find yourself in these pages. And for those who read this book whom I don't know, if you fit the description of how I describe my friends, then come along for the ride. We would probably be friends anyway. But enough about you for a moment . . . I want to talk about me and my problem.

Here it is in a nutshell: I love God, and I know beyond a shadow of a doubt that He is real. He has proven that to me for decades. That is not my problem.

My problem is that I love my friends, and many of them do not know God, at least in any way that they have told me about. So, the problem is this: I want them to know Him and know that He is real. I want them to have a relationship with Him and know how incredible that is.

So why is that a problem? Simple . . . I often do not know how to tell them.

Perhaps you've felt this tension too—wanting to share something meaningful without risking a relationship that matters to you.

PRAYER

Lord, You know how much I want to share You with the people I love. I want to share the most important thing in my life but some of these relationships are fragile. Give me wisdom to know when to speak and when to just love. And when I do speak, let me do it with the kind of gentleness that makes people curious rather than defensive. Thank You for caring about my friends even more than I do. In Jesus' name. Amen.

2

He Is Not Far from You

God did this so that they would seek him and perhaps reach out for him and find him, though he is not far from any one of us.

—Acts 17:27

Think back to a moment when you felt unexpectedly close to something greater than yourself.

One night, as a ten-year-old at camp in North Carolina, I felt a stirring in my soul that has never gone away. The night had been a regular camp night . . . with counselors and cabin-mates at the big bonfire . . . doing camp-like things. It was a "lightly" Christian camp, not an in-your-face, overbearing type of religious camp. Mainly it was a sports and wildlife experience for four weeks of fun and some attempt by the counselors at spiritual and character development.

That week had been one of a difficult-to-explain heightening of my love for God. I had always had a strong consciousness of God from early childhood . . . I somehow knew He was there. He showed Himself in me in ways I can't really explain. But this particular camp experience led me to a little mountainside chapel as I was out for a hike, where I had an experience that I remember as if it were yesterday. As I sat there in silence, I was overcome with a movement in my heart. I felt Him drawing me to Him . . . it was kind of overwhelming, in a good way. The love was so strong that I felt for Him. As I sat there, I told Him that I would do whatever He wanted me to do with my life. I had been moved by an Invisible Force that I knew was real and loving. I was sure of that.

Your own mountainside chapel might look different from mine—perhaps it's your garden, a quiet room, or even a crowded street where you suddenly felt that stirring in your soul.

PRAYER

God, sometimes I forget how close You really are. Thank You for those sacred moments when You make yourself known—not with thunder and lightning, but in quiet stirrings of the heart. You're never far from any of us. Help me stay alert to Your Presence today, even in the ordinary moments. Let me feel that same wonder I've felt before, knowing You're right here, waiting to be found. In Jesus' name. Amen.

3

When Grace Finally Makes Sense

God made him who had no sin to be sin for us, so that in him we might become the righteousness of God. —2 Corinthians 5:21

Sometimes the most familiar truths hit us in fresh ways when we least expect it.

I had heard the "gospel" message before, but this time it pierced me more deeply.

The camp counselor said the gospel was a simple message that was like this: Think of if you committed a crime, and went to court, and were found guilty by the judge. You are standing in front of the bench, and he pronounces the verdict: guilty as charged. And then he pronounces the penalty. You know you cannot pay it. You are guilty, and you are convicted. You must pay the fine. And you also realize that you cannot afford the price.

Then, right at that moment, the judge says, "I will come down and stand in your place and pay the fine for you if you want me to. You may go free if you want to accept my offer."

The camp counselor then said, "That is what Jesus did for us. He paid our fine, and if we accept His payment, His death on the cross for us, we can go free and be pronounced 'not guilty.'" We can be forever forgiven by God for everything we have ever done, or ever will do. It has been paid for, if we accept it.

Where are you standing today—in front of the bench awaiting judgment, or ready to accept the payment that's already been made on your behalf?

Somehow the simplicity of that moved me in a different way than it had ever before. I realized the love that I had felt from God was from a loving Father, not mad at me for being "bad," and not ready to zap me for any mistake. I understood in a much deeper way.

PRAYER

Father, thank You for making Your love so clear through Jesus. Like that judge stepping down from the bench, You didn't just pronounce the verdict—You provided the solution. When I'm tempted to think I need to earn Your love or that You're keeping score of my failures, help me remember this simple truth: You've already paid my fine. You're not mad at me; You're my loving Father who went to incredible lengths to bring me home. Thank You for such amazing grace. In Jesus' name. Amen.

4

When You're Scared to Share What Matters Most

For I am not ashamed of the gospel, because it is the power of God that brings salvation to everyone who believes. —Romans 1:16

What's the most important thing in your life that you find difficult to talk about?

I felt the pain of knowing that my best friend did not know God . . . but I felt squeamish about how to tell him. After all, we were much more concerned with being cool and tough and winning games and trophies than being one of those weird religious types. So, I had never talked to him about it. And that night, I cried with my camp counselor in front of the fireplace back at the lodge. I needed to know how to get out of the dilemma of carrying around such an incredible Reality that I knew my friend would want to know, and at the same time being too afraid to talk about it.

That tension between knowing something wonderful and fearing others' reactions is something we all face in different ways.

Well, since that time, a lot has happened. And I have seen way more of how real God is, and what He can do. And this book is my attempt to put my journey with God into words . . . for one purpose: I want my friends to know that God is real. "You might think I am crazy, but this is why I believe, and why I want you to have a relationship with Him, too."

PRAYER

God, sometimes carrying this amazing truth about You feels so heavy—knowing You're real, knowing how much You love us, but feeling stuck when it comes to sharing it. Please take my fear of what others might think and replace it with confidence in Your love. Give me courage to be honest about what You mean to me, even when I'm scared of looking uncool or weird. Help me care more about my friends knowing You than about looking foolish. In Jesus' name. Amen.

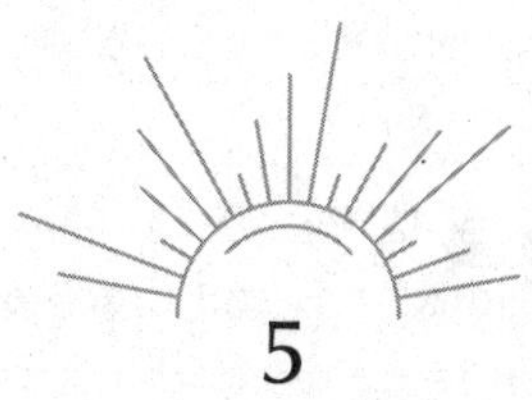

5

Got Questions? Yeah, Me Too.

This is what the LORD says, he who made the earth, the LORD who formed it and established it—the LORD is his name: "Call to me and I will answer you and tell you great and unsearchable things you do not know." —Jeremiah 33:2–3

What questions about faith have kept you awake at night or made you hesitate to go deeper?

There are a lot of obstacles to faith. I had them myself after I decided to get more serious about my faith later in life, so it is easy for me to understand when others have those questions.

Life has so many dilemmas that make it hard to believe in a good God, and the people who sell the God message can sometimes be so weird and obnoxious that we just feel like "If this faith were true, then all of that crap would not exist that surrounds it." As I used to think when I was a kid, *I like God; I just don't like His friends.*

Of course, not all Christians are "that kind." So many are awesome people who do incredible things. They give of their time, talents, and resources to make the world better, alleviating poverty, suffering, and much more. But as I talk to people who do not share my faith, their experiences with some believers are often a big obstacle to God. The fascinating thing is: the religious people that you and I both struggle with are the same ones Jesus didn't get along with, either.

So, come along with me as I share my experience, my questions, and the answers that satisfied my doubts.

Your doubts and questions are not obstacles to faith—they might be the very path that leads you to a more authentic relationship with God.

Along the way, my hope is that you get more than answers. I hope you have encounters with God that draw you closer to Him and His love.

PRAYER

God, I'm bringing You my questions. Thank You that You're not scared of them. Thank You that You invite me to think deeply and search honestly. Help me look past the weird religious stuff that gets in the way and find You—the real You. Show me who You really are. Thank You that You're big enough to handle my doubts and loving enough to walk with me through them. In Jesus' name. Amen.

6

What If You Could Love God Without All the Religious Stuff?

"You are the light of the world. A town built on a hill cannot be hidden. Neither do people light a lamp and put it under a bowl. Instead they put it on its stand, and it gives light to everyone in the house. In the same way, let your light shine before others, that they may see your good deeds and glorify your Father in heaven."

—Matthew 5:14–16

Have you ever felt that connecting with God shouldn't require so many religious trappings? Perhaps you've wondered if there's a way to have an authentic relationship with God that feels true to who you really are, rather than fitting someone else's mold of what faith should look like.

My parents introduced me to faith early in life, and they were active in a local Methodist church. They taught me that life was always lived before God, but they did so in a pretty low-key traditional way of attending church on Sunday and showing one's faith through service to others.

My mother would say bedtime prayers with me each night, in the tradition of "Now I lay me down to sleep." My father could be seen reading his Bible and attending church regularly, but we had nothing like family devotions or that kind of overt "faith" training. That was left to the Sunday school teachers. Faith wasn't spoken about as much as it was lived and assumed.

My father was a "guy's guy," a lot more fun than some of the more "religious" parents of my friends. A World War II first sergeant, Daddy was pretty tough, but he was also loving and really funny. Yet you always knew that he stood for things; he had strong principles, and one of those was his faith. He was serious about it, just not very loud about it.

So, in that way, I did grow up in a Christian family, just not in an over-the-top way.

Our home was a gathering place for all kinds of folks. My parents were really good people, and everyone loved them. It was normal in our small town of Vicksburg, Mississippi, for everyone to serve others and take care of them.

PRAYER

Lord, thank You for the people who've shown me that following You doesn't have to look "churchy" or weird. Help me find my own authentic way of walking with You—not copying someone else's style, but living out my faith in ways that feel real and true. Help me care more about loving people than looking religious. In Jesus' name. Amen.

7

Finding God in Secret Acts of Service

Suppose a brother or a sister is without clothes and daily food. If one of you says to them, "Go in peace; keep warm and well fed," but does nothing about their physical needs, what good is it? In the same way, faith by itself, if it is not accompanied by action, is dead.

—James 2:15–17

When was the last time you did something kind without needing recognition for it?

Here's a favorite story that shows how my father lived out faith more than talked about it. He was in his twenties when World War II started, and he had enlisted in the National Guard. They gave him an IQ test, and he scored in the genius level, even though he had dropped out of school to support his family in the eighth grade.

The interesting thing about the men he served with is that they were all artists, sculptors, and set designers from

Hollywood . . . non-soldiers who had been recruited to build the models that the generals used to plan battles. They built rooms of mountain ranges, cities, and other topography so that the strategies could be formed. These young men were displaced in England, away from home, separated from their families, lonely, and often just feeling lost.

One night my father went into town and got into a craps game (as I said, he was Christian but not overly religious) and won what amounted to a lot of money. He went out and secretly bought a restaurant. Since this was not permissible for him as a foreign serviceman, he found an older couple to run the place.

Each week, he would drive into the country and trade tea to farmers for chickens and potatoes. Then, he would have the couple close the restaurant on Saturday night and throw a party for the US soldiers with fried chicken and french fries. It was all free, and they could bring their dates. Just a gift from an old English couple to the American soldiers. No one ever knew who was behind it all. When he left England, he gave the restaurant to the old couple as a gift.

What would it look like in your life today to express your faith through quiet acts of generosity that might never be traced back to you?

This story exemplifies the way that faith was shown to me by my parents as a kid. It was real but lived out much more in giving and caring for others than being overtly religious.

PRAYER

Lord, thanks for reminding me that faith isn't just about Sunday mornings or speaking the right religious words. Help me notice the lonely, the homesick, the discouraged—like those soldiers far from home. Give me Your heart to see beyond the surface and Your wisdom to find practical ways to show love, whether anyone sees it or not. Make my faith as real as that restaurant full of fried chicken and friendship. In Jesus' name. Amen.

8

You Can Meet with God in the Quiet Moments

You have searched me, LORD, and you know me . . . You discern my going out and my lying down; you are familiar with all my ways . . . Such knowledge is too wonderful for me, too lofty for me to attain. Where can I go from your Spirit? Where can I flee from your presence? If I go up to the heavens, you are there; if I make my bed in the depths, you are there.

—Psalms 139:1, 3, 6–8

Where do you experience God most naturally in your everyday life?

For much of my early life, my faith was pretty much private and silent, but still real to me. I always believed in God. From early on, I just somehow knew God was there . . . I even felt Him at various times. He seemed pretty constant and close.

I saw Him in everything, especially the beauty of nature and creation. It made sense that Someone made the beauty of the dark woods I hunted and rode horses in; of the lakes I swam, fished, and water-skied in; and of the smells of spring, especially the grass after a downpour. I was a golfer from early in life, and I will always have the smell of fresh green grass deep in my soul. I knew God made that.

My mother worked in the family business, and many of my days as a kid were spent alone when I was not engaged in sports or play. Whether in the woods, horseback riding, on my bike, hunting or fishing, or on the golf course I spent a lot of time alone and with God, talking to Him about life.

Think about your own spaces where you sense God's Presence—whether in nature, in moments of solitude, or in the beauty of ordinary things that stir something deeper in your soul. Wherever it is, you might decide to prioritize spending time in that space.

PRAYER

God, in this busy world where noise and distractions surround me, help me carve out spaces to simply be with You. Open my eyes to see Your fingerprints in creation and my heart to feel Your Presence in the quiet moments. Give me the childlike faith to talk with You, like a trusted friend. In Jesus' name. Amen.

9

When You Feel Like You Don't Fit In

Am I now trying to win the approval of human beings, or of God? Or am I trying to please people? If I were still trying to please people, I would not be a servant of Christ. —Galatians 1:10

Have you ever felt caught between different worlds, not quite belonging in either one?

If so, I can relate.

Watching my parents live their lives in our community and hanging out with God as a companion and recipient of my existential questions—represented the extent of my "spiritual life" as a child. As I grew older, I became aware of something that troubled me: there were two groups of people with whom my spiritual life did not align.

First, there were the hardcore church people, with whom I did not identify at all, and they were very different from my family. They seemed to have a lot of rules . . . like not being able to go to dances or movies, or play poker, or bet on rounds of golf. Or, for some, even playing golf on

Sunday. I always felt judged by them . . . and at the same time, felt like I was sort of like them, as we both believed in God. I think I was like my dad . . . he loved God but kind of poked fun at some of the overly religious types. I wonder if you've ever found yourself drawn to authentic faith but uncomfortable with some of the religious packaging it often comes in?

Second, there were the people who did not have anything to do with God that I could see. In some ways, I could relate to them more. They did all the activities that I loved and were much more chill. They would even go water-skiing on Sunday! But they would also engage in pursuits I knew my parents wouldn't approve of—although frequently, I might be present, just not participating.

The dilemma of being spiritual deep in my heart and at the same time not being able to fully identify with "religion" or "church types" was the predominant theme of my early years. I wanted to talk to my best friend, who was a pretty wild kid, about God, and yet I feared he would see me as "one of them." I didn't know what to do with friends like him, and sometimes I still don't. I held on to my secret spiritual life, unable to be one of those religious types, and so I felt like I had no place to land, like a spiritual wanderer without a true home. So, it was pretty much just me and God.

PRAYER

God, sometimes I feel caught between worlds—not "religious enough" for some and too spiritual for others. Thank You that You see past these human categories straight into my heart. Help me remember that my relationship with You doesn't have to look like anyone else's. Give me courage to be authentic about my faith, even when I feel like I don't quite fit in. Thank You for accepting me exactly as I am. In Jesus' name. Amen.

10

When God Gives You a Different Plan

"Do not fear, for I have redeemed you; I have summoned you by your name; you are mine. When you pass through the waters, I will be with you; and when you pass through the rivers, they will not sweep over you. When you walk through the fire, you will not be burned; the flames will not set you ablaze." —Isaiah 43:1–2

Has life—or God—ever taken you in a direction you never would have chosen, but somehow turned out better than you could have planned?

There was one overt "God event" in my early years that is important in understanding my spiritual evolution. One Sunday morning, when I was almost four years old, I was sitting on the floor at Sunday school when my left leg began to hurt badly. It got worse until my parents had to be called in. I remember they took me home, and there was a flurry of activity going on in the house as they were calling doctors. I vividly remember a very ominous dark feeling that day.

Later that day I was hospitalized, and the doctors began working to find out what was wrong with me. My parents would tell me later that I would scream in pain for many nights, and how frightened they were. I was in agony, and they felt helpless. The doctors did every test they knew to do, and I remained in the hospital for some time.

At some point, the doctors were considering amputation of my leg, and my mother had taken me to the appointment with her best friend, Emmett. As they waited, my mother heard a voice, saying, "Leave here, and take him to Ochsner in New Orleans." Ochsner was the big training hospital of the South at that time. It was the place you went when all else failed.

My mother was certain because of the Voice she had clearly heard. She took me home and somehow convinced my otherwise levelheaded father to drive 225 miles with no doctor, no plan, no referral . . . just a direction straight "from God."

Maybe you've been there—you've faced a situation where you felt something guiding you in a different direction than the conventional wisdom would have you go.

At Ochsner, I was "randomly" assigned to Dr. Mary Sherman. She examined me and said, "There will be no amputation. I know exactly what this is and how to treat it." As it turned out, she was one of the most heralded international bone specialists in the world, specifically trained in treating this disorder. Just the right one . . . not a coincidence.

PRAYER

God, when I'm facing impossible situations, help me recognize Your voice through all the noise and fear. Give me the courage to follow Your direction even when it doesn't make sense to others. Thank You that You see the whole picture when I can only see part of it. Thank You that You still make a way where there seems to be no way. Help me trust that You're working behind the scenes, arranging details I can't even imagine. In Jesus' name. Amen.

11

God Is There in the Hard Times

"Be strong and courageous . . . The LORD himself goes before you and will be with you; he will never leave you nor forsake you. Do not be afraid; do not be discouraged." —Deuteronomy 31:7–8

When have you experienced something so difficult it changed how you saw yourself and the world around you?

Looking back, I can't tell you specifically how God sending my mother out of the wrong doctor's office and to the right one figured in my early faith. I just knew from my parents that God had intervened in my life, and His care became part of my life narrative—that God was there and that He looks out for us in hard times.

I learned early what trauma was like . . . going from an active almost four-year-old to one day suddenly being told I could not walk anymore and would be in a wheelchair! It happened out of nowhere. I screamed: "Why can't I walk? Let me walk!"

It was a really difficult time, for close to two years. Being in severe pain . . . sitting on the sidelines at birthday parties while other children rode the pony, feeling like something was wrong with me . . . walking down stairs on my crutches and leg braces and tripping and falling, stabbed by my broken crutches . . . being called "Crip" and having flashbacks of scary X-ray machines and medical procedures.

Perhaps you've experienced your own version of those moments—when life's pain becomes visible to others, leaving you feeling exposed and vulnerable.

For me, I was different somehow. Flawed. Ashamed.

It was a difficult period for me and our family and one that would have other psychological and emotional ramifications in my life. But the spiritual imprinting on me was powerful . . . that when there is tragedy and life is no longer like it was before, He is there.

PRAYER

Father God, when life feels overwhelming and I'm struggling with pain, remind me of Your constant Presence. Help me feel Your comfort when I'm sitting on the sidelines of life. Thank You for being there in my hard times, for guiding me to the right people and places, and for writing my story with purpose, even when I can't understand it. In Jesus' name. Amen.

12

Learning to Let Go of Your Plans

Many are the plans in a person's heart, but it is the LORD's purpose that prevails. —Proverbs 19:21

What happens when the future you've been planning and working toward suddenly falls apart?

Playing junior golf in Mississippi in my high school years was exciting. I was being recruited by different schools when I got an invite from the coach at Southern Methodist University to come to Dallas. I accepted the invitation to visit and play with the coach.

Upon arriving, I was stunned to find out the coach had resigned abruptly. An interim coach was put in, and since my promised scholarship was only partial the first semester, the interim coach said he was going to hit reset and we newbies would have to qualify for the team. I agreed to stay and play the qualifier. There were a lot of good players trying to qualify, and only two spots for the team. I made it.

Later that fall, I injured my wrist, and my play was hampered throughout the rest of the year. Through the spring of my sophomore year, my wrist pain worsened. I fought it, playing well at some times but not well at others. Finally, after fighting it as long as I could, I called my dad and Coach Stewart and told them I was going to hang it up. It felt pointless to continue to fight trying to play when with every backswing I did not know if I would have a knife shoot through my wrist or not.

My dream and my lifelong passion in golf up to that point was now over. Dead in the water, and I felt worse than dead myself.

Perhaps you're facing your own version of this right now—a dream slipping away, a path forward suddenly blocked, or a passion you can no longer pursue.

PRAYER

Father, I have grieved the death of dreams. When everything in me wants to keep fighting, give me wisdom to know when it's time to let go. Help me believe You're not finished writing my story, even when the chapter ends differently than I planned. Help me to know that what I really need is Your unfailing love. In Jesus' name. Amen.

13

Learning to Live with Loss

The LORD is close to the brokenhearted and saves those who are crushed in spirit. The righteous person may have many troubles, but the LORD delivers him from them all. —Psalms 34:18–1

What meaningful activities, relationships, or identities have you had to say goodbye to?

To lose golf was to lose what I thought my life was about. To say I was depressed would be an understatement. It also had a lot to do with losing something special with my dad. He had started me playing with him when I was a really little kid. It was something we shared deeply; he would always come to my tournaments and get more nervous than I would.

Once, I was invited to play in the St. Jude Classic pro-am in Memphis as a teenager. I remember going on to the range to warm up and was slotted between Lee Trevino and Gary Player, and Jack Nicklaus was a few players away. I thought my dad was going to faint, seeing his kid hitting balls with all of the great players of the time. I shot six under par for the last sixteen holes, winning the pro-am with partner Larry Ziegler. It was one of my fondest memories with my dad and golf. Losing my golf game meant losing something very special with him, and it hit me hard to tell him I was giving it up.

Your losses might look different from mine, but that feeling of emptiness when something central to your identity is gone—that's something many of us understand all too well.

At the same time that I lost my golf game, my girlfriend and I broke up. So, here I was, twenty years old and, in my mind, a total washout. Depressed, and with no idea what my future held or what I even wanted to do. Those were very dark days.

I know now, as a psychologist, that not having a life purpose at that age was not the cause of my depression. It was the losses I had recently sustained that were sending me into an abyss. What I did not know at the time was that those losses were cracking a not very strong foundation of being a pretty wounded person underneath it all. My obsessive pursuits of sports and academic achievements were covering a lot of pain that I had never faced from my growing-up years.

PRAYER

Father, sometimes it feels like everything's falling apart—like one loss leads to another until I don't even know who I am anymore.

Thank You for staying close when I'm hurting. Help me trust that You see beyond the surface of my losses to the deeper healing I need. Give me courage to face the pain I've been running from or covering up. Remind me that even in my darkest moments, You haven't forgotten me. In Jesus' name. Amen.

14

When God Doesn't Show Up

How long, LORD? Will you forget me forever? How long will you hide your face from me? How long must I wrestle with my thoughts and day after day have sorrow in my heart? —Psalms 13:1–2

Have you ever reached out to God in desperate need, only to be met with what feels like silence?

One Sunday afternoon I was sitting on my bed in my dorm room at SMU, staring into nothing, everything dark. There was a merry-go-round of questions going through my head. How do you get undepressed when nothing you try works? How would I make a living and achieve "success"? The questions seemed to be a whir in my head at that moment.

I looked across the room and my eyes somehow were drawn to my Bible. I had taken it to school but had not opened it since I had arrived. Something was drawing me to that book.

I went over and got it and sat back down. Not knowing where to turn, I randomly opened it up. I looked down at the page, and a passage sort of leaped off the page, "Seek first the kingdom of God and His righteousness and all these things shall be added to you" (Matt. 6:33 NKJV).

Right as I was worrying about "all these things," it said that if I would seek God, all of this would work out? Really?

I had tried everything else, so . . . why not? *Okay,* I thought. *I'll try this.*

I walked over to the little chapel across from the dorm. I walked to the altar, knelt down, and said: "God, I really don't even know if You are really there. But I need help. Please . . . help me. And if You do, I will do whatever You want me to do."

And then . . . nothing. Nothing happened. Silence. It was devastating.

I felt even more hopeless. God had not shown up.

PRAYER

God, I'm not sure if You're even listening. But something in me still reaches for You, even if it's just out of desperation. I don't need a dramatic sign or a supernatural encounter—I just need to know You're there. Help me to keep seeking You, even when it feels like I'm talking to empty air. Give me the courage to wait, and the faith to believe You're working even when I can't see it. In Jesus' name. Amen.

15

You Can Find Hope When You Keep Coming Back

The LORD is good to those whose hope is in him, to the one who seeks him; it is good to wait quietly for the salvation of the LORD. . . . For no one is cast off by the Lord forever. Though he brings grief, he will show compassion, so great is his unfailing love. For he does not willingly bring affliction or grief to anyone.

—Lamentations 3:25–26, 31–33

What happens when your prayers go unanswered? That was my situation, and I wasn't sure what was next.

I vividly remember receiving a phone call from my fraternity brother Ed Atkinson. He said something like: "I don't know what made me think of you, but I did, so I am calling to tell you we are starting a Bible study at the fraternity house, and I wanted to see if you would want to come." I thought, *This has to be a sign.* Little did I know how that call would forever change my life.

I went to the Bible study, led by Ed's brother-in-law, Bill. I knew I needed to talk to Bill more about what I had been going through, so I asked him to meet me for lunch. I told him how depressed I had been, and how it seemed like God hadn't been doing anything when I prayed for help. He just said, "Keep coming to the study. Sometimes God has His own timing, and He uses people, too. He can use the group to help you as you learn more about Him."

That seemed like such a cop-out. I wanted God to do something dramatic—write across the sky, touch me supernaturally, show me what to do! Didn't He see I was desperate? All I got was "Keep coming . . . God uses people, too." But I had no other choice, so I kept coming back.

What small, seemingly ordinary connections in your life right now might actually be God's answer arriving in unexpected packaging?

PRAYER

Lord, I'm tired of waiting for dramatic signs. Help me trust that You're working in ways I might not expect. Give me the courage to keep showing up, even when I don't feel like it. Thank You for being patient with my impatience. Help me see the small ways You're moving in my life today. In Jesus' name. Amen.

16

When Your Questions Meet God's Answers

"Ask and it will be given to you; seek and you will find; knock and the door will be opened to you. For everyone who asks receives; the one who seeks finds; and to the one who knocks, the door will be opened." —Matthew 7:7–8

What questions about faith have kept you awake at night or made you hesitate to trust God completely? You might have doubts connected to science, suffering, or why God seems silent in certain areas of your life.

It took me awhile, but I finally learned the most important thing. It's what I want you to know. *God answers our prayers and our questions.* I had questions about science and the Bible, evolution, the Flood, quantum physics, astronomy and cosmology, biology, philosophy, archaeology, theology, the existence of evil, pain and suffering, and the like.

I found that there were astrophysicists, PhD professors in biology, cosmology, geology, archaeology, and all of the sciences who believed for scientific reasons that science did not go against their faith but in fact *proved* their faith. After studying extensively, my questions dissolved. I found out, from scientists themselves, that there is no scientific reason to not have faith.

Science can only observe what already exists . . . it cannot observe what does not exist, nor can it observe or know where what does exist came from. It can build theories and have "faith" in its theories, but it cannot know any more about where it all came from than just to have its own "faith" that the material world was "eternal." It cannot explain why the material or physical matter of the universe always existed, or if it didn't, how it suddenly did. Nor can it explain why the intricate interworkings of everything that exists works together as well as it does.

I was finding out that what the Bible said was true: "'You will seek me and find me when you seek me with all your heart'" (Jer. 29:13 NIV).

Each step of the way, as I sought Him, He gave me the answers I needed or showed me that I didn't really need them after all. I just needed Him. But I still had what felt like a much bigger problem.

I was still depressed.

And two things were becoming clear to me: God was answering prayers, *and* not answering them. He was showing me that He was real, but not really healing my depression.

PRAYER

Lord, I'm bringing You my biggest questions today. Thank You that You're big enough for every doubt and patient enough for every question. Give me wisdom as I search for answers and help me recognize Your voice when You respond. Most of all, help me find You in the process. In Jesus' name. Amen.

17

God Is Alive and Will Enter and Intervene in Your Life

"See, I am doing a new thing! Now it springs up; do you not perceive it? I am making a way in the wilderness and streams in the wasteland." —Isaiah 43:19

Have you ever wished you could see concrete proof that God is active in today's world?

The more I learned about God, the more I sought Him. I read everything I could put my hands on about the evidence for faith in Jesus, and also about spiritual growth. Some of the most powerful reading I did was about the reality of God's being there for people. I found a whole new world of literature that I never knew existed: spiritual biographies and testimonies. I found out I was not imagining the reality of His intervening in our worlds . . . countless others had testimonies of the same.

Might there be stories of God's intervention unfolding around you right now that you haven't recognized as His handiwork?

One of the first that really affected me was *The Cross and the Switchblade* by David Wilkerson. It was the story of a small-town preacher in Pennsylvania whom God visited in the middle of the night and told to go to New York City to rescue some gang members accused of horrible crimes. I had no idea God did supernatural things still . . . I knew the Bible talked about them, but I had never heard much about those happening today.

Another book I remember reading was *God's Smuggler* by Brother Andrew. It was the story of how he smuggled Bibles into communist countries and the miracles of God's protection and intervention. These books and many others showed me something I didn't understand before—that *God is alive and will enter and intervene in our lives.*

PRAYER

God, sometimes I forget You're still doing miracles today. Open my eyes to see You working in my world. I know You can guide me too. Help me notice the small ways You show up in my everyday life and give me the courage to step out when You call. Make me aware of Your Presence today. In Jesus' name. Amen.

18

Finding Hope in the Dark

I waited patiently for the LORD; he turned to me and heard my cry. He lifted me out of the slimy pit, out of the mud and mire; he set my feet on a rock and gave me a firm place to stand. He put a new song in my mouth, a hymn of praise to our God.

—Psalms 40:1–3

When was the last time you felt stuck in a dark place with no clear way out?

While growth in my faith was going well, finding my way out of depression was not. I went home to Mississippi from Dallas for the summer, and decided that since so much of my pain was associated with losses while at SMU, and I didn't know what I wanted to study, I would transfer to Ole Miss. I thought a change of scenery might help something click. In retrospect, I was running from the pain, which was probably not a bad idea. As summer continued, everything got worse. Even concentrating was difficult. I was working as a bank teller, and sometimes could not focus enough to do my work. One day it came to a head when I mistakenly wrapped fifty fifty-dollar bills in a one-dollar bill wrapper and gave it to a woman making a withdrawal. She won the "pick a depressed teller" lottery and never came back, and I lost my job.

During that time of struggle, I experienced my first supernatural experience. In a despondent moment after losing my job, I drove to my family's lake house, where I used to talk to God as a teenager. What I didn't know was that He was looking to be close to me.

I was driving on the deeply wooded road to the lake, talking to God, when He came into my entire being in the most powerful way. It felt like I was being supercharged with energy, lifting me up into a high I had never felt. As a psychologist, if I heard this from someone, I might think they were having a manic episode, but I wasn't. My thinking, impulse control, and mental status were all fine, and afterward the depression was still around. I knew it was God touching me, showing me He was with me. It was so strong that I remember telling Him, "Okay! That is enough! Stop!" It felt as if it would be too much if it were any stronger. After a while, it just left. I went back home to my depressed, struggling world. But I had been touched by Him, and somehow . . . encouraged.

Perhaps you're in your own version of that deeply wooded road right now—a place where you need God to show up and remind you that you're not alone, even if your circumstances don't immediately change.

PRAYER

This story reminds me that You see me in my struggles and You're actively seeking me out. Thank You that I don't have to have it all together to come to You. Help me remember that You're right here with me, ready to meet me wherever I am. In Jesus' name. Amen.

19

He's with You Even When He Doesn't Fix It

Even though I walk through the darkest valley, I will fear no evil, for you are with me; your rod and your staff, they comfort me.

—Psalms 23:4

Do you struggle with the disconnect between knowing God is with you and yet not seeing Him resolve your difficult situation?

I get that.

It was amazing to experience God's touch so strongly during my drive to the lake. Yet it was confusing to still be in a bad place. God didn't heal me at that moment. But I learned a valuable twofold lesson: God is with us even when things are really bad. Just because things are bad doesn't mean He's not with us. And just because He is with us doesn't mean He removes all the bad stuff right then. I later saw He says this in the Bible many times.

I was learning something important that was breaking through my immature spiritual life . . . God allows us to go through pain, and pain doesn't mean He doesn't care or isn't with us. I couldn't deny reality—I knew He was there.

Where in your life right now do you need to embrace this paradox—that God can be powerfully present without instantly removing your pain?

Later at Ole Miss registration, overwhelmed with depression and anxiety, I could barely concentrate enough to fill out the forms. Suddenly, a man walked up to me and said, "God is with you, and one day you're going to be a great man of God, serving Him in big ways." I looked at him like he was crazy—I could barely get through the day. But it was like God saw me and told me again, "Keep walking. I am with you." That was enough to keep me going one more day.

PRAYER

God, I'm struggling with the fact that You feel close but my circumstances haven't changed. Sometimes I wonder why You don't just fix everything. Help me find comfort in Your Presence, even when the answers don't come. Thank You for the small reminders You send my way—the unexpected encouragement, the quiet whispers that tell me I'm not alone. Help me trust Your timing, even when I don't understand it. In Jesus' name. Amen.

20

God Is Closer Than You Think

You will weep no more. How gracious he will be when you cry for help! As soon as he hears, he will answer you. Although the Lord gives you the bread of adversity and the water of affliction, your teachers will be hidden no more; with your own eyes you will see them. Whether you turn to the right or to the left, your ears will hear a voice behind you, saying, "This is the way; walk in it."

—Isaiah 30:19–21

When have you experienced the unique confusion of needing divine guidance for a situation that seemed to have no clear solution?

As fall approached, a revival was taking place at a church in my town. Unlike my regular Methodist church, this place believed in God healing people through prayer. I went, hoping to get "zapped." While I kept to myself during the service, I sensed the pastor truly believed in a God who would intervene in our lives.

Soon after, in a really bad place, I prayed for help and felt strongly I needed to talk to this pastor. The church was closed, but I remembered my dad had mentioned he lived somewhere north of the city. Desperate, I prayed, "God, take me to him."

I began driving, and at each intersection, I felt prompted to turn left or right. After about twenty minutes deep into a subdivision, I made one final turn. Suddenly, the atmosphere in my car completely changed. I felt an incredible divine Presence surrounding me. I stopped instantly and looked up to see a mailbox marked "Rev. Jenkins." I had been led directly to the pastor's house.

Have you ever experienced one of those moments when the pieces fell into place so perfectly that it couldn't be mere coincidence—a divine intersection that felt orchestrated by something beyond yourself?

I knocked, and Reverend Jenkins listened to my troubles. Though I hoped he would make everything better through healing or counseling, what happened instead was significant. I broke down so completely that evening he called my parents to get me. While at the end of his skills, he wisely recognized I needed psychiatric help, that I was chemically depressed and needed a doctor. He started me on the path toward proper treatment.

That overwhelming presence in the car taught me something powerful: God is far more real and near than we realize, and He will intervene to help us.

PRAYER

Lord, sometimes I feel lost and don't know where to turn. Thank You that You're closer than I think, even when I can't feel You. Help me trust that You hear my prayers and will guide me—even if the help comes in unexpected ways. Give me the courage to follow Your promptings and the humility to accept help through others, whether that's a pastor, a doctor, or a friend. Thank You for being a God who shows up in real, tangible ways. In Jesus' name. Amen.

21

When God Shows Up Unexpectedly

When you pass through the waters, I will be with you; and when you pass through the rivers, they will not sweep over you. When you walk through the fire, you will not be burned; the flames will not set you ablaze. —Isaiah 43:2

Perhaps you've experienced a moment when everything seemed to be going wrong, yet somehow you felt an inexplicable peace or presence that couldn't be explained away.

My parents decided I needed psychiatric help and took me back to the Ochsner clinic in New Orleans. The psychiatrist was inept yet grandiosely confident. He completely misdiagnosed me, put me on the wrong medicine, and started down a course of therapy that had very little to do with what I was dealing with. He just did not understand me. The medicine was producing significant side effects and making me worse. I felt so abandoned by God, and by my parents as well. Here I was, alone in a hospital 225 miles from home, missing the beginning of the school year, having no plan and no hope.

One bright spot—further supernatural evidence that God was at work in my life, guiding and protecting me—stands out in my memory. My sister, who lived in New Orleans at the time, came to visit one day, and we went out to the French Quarter just to get me out and about. We were about to enter an antique bookstore when it happened. *God's Presence fell all over us.* I know it sounds crazy. It was *so* powerful . . . He was enveloping us there on the sidewalk. I knew for sure it was Him.

I said to Sharon, "Stop . . . we need to pray." And I just said, "God, I know You are here . . . please let me know why You are here and what to do." I didn't get any answer when I prayed, just His Presence.

PRAYER

Father, sometimes I feel so alone. But You get it. Thank You for those surprising moments when Your Presence wraps around me like a warm blanket, proving You haven't forgotten me. When everything feels wrong and I'm far from home, help me remember You're right here, turning my fires and floods into testimonies of Your faithfulness. In Jesus' name. Amen.

22

When You Need Power You Don't Have

The LORD will protect you from all evil; He will keep your life. The LORD will guard your going out and your coming in from this time forth and forever. —Psalms 121:7–8 AMP

You try to be strong, self-sufficient. Then you find yourself in a situation where you need courage or strength beyond your own. How does that feel? What do you do?

After sensing God's Presence outside of a bookstore in the French Quarter, my sister and I walked in and began to look around. I could still feel God's Presence around me as we wandered through the bookshelves. I noticed a section of spiritual books. The first one I saw was a book by Hal Lindsey. When I stopped, a very creepy man dressed in all black said with a very scary tone, "Ahhh . . . so you are a Satanist?"

What I had not seen was the book Lindsey had written called *Satan Is Alive and Well on Planet Earth*. When I stopped to look at it, this Satanist saw me and figured I was on his team.

I immediately felt very empowered and emboldened in some strange way . . . and said, “No! I am a Christian!”

When I said that, he drew back and recoiled . . . and said in the most hideous voice, “Oh! You are from the wrong side!” and then quickly almost slithered away.

Sharon was getting freaked out, and grabbed me, saying, “Let’s get out of here.”

I had learned another lesson: when I needed Him, He showed up. There was not a doubt that I was encountering some dark power that day, and God protected me from something I can only imagine.

You might not face someone dressed in black today, but you’ll likely encounter situations where you need power beyond your natural abilities—and that’s *exactly* when God shows up.

PRAYER

Lord, sometimes I get caught off guard by darkness I didn’t see coming. Thank You that You are already there before I even know I need You. Help me remember that Your Presence isn’t just comforting—it’s powerful. Give me boldness to stand firm in my faith, knowing You always have my back. In Jesus’ name. Amen.

23

When God Sends Help Through a Friend

A friend loves at all times, and a brother is born for a time of adversity. —Proverbs 17:17

When was the last time someone called or reached out to you at exactly the right moment?

I was in the hospital, waiting and hoping for Dr. Didn't Know What He Was Doing to help me and then . . . it happened. A nurse came to me and said I had a phone call. It was my friend Edward . . . the same friend who had invited me to that Bible study back at SMU. He had found out from my parents that I was in the hospital and said that he was coming to visit me. I suddenly felt like God had not forgotten me. Edward calling seemed like a ray of light through the darkness. It was like God's calvary was coming, since he was the one who had started it all after my initial calling out to God.

Consider who in your life right now might be that "Edward" for you—or who might need you to be their Edward, making the call that feels like a lifeline in their darkness.

Edward arrived the next day. In his typical take-no-prisoners mode, he decided, "these people are idiots. We need to get you to someone who understands your faith and can help you medically." So, he called his brother-in-law Bill, the seminary student who had led that first Bible study at the Beta house at SMU. Bill was taking counseling courses from Dr. Frank Minirth, and Edward thought maybe Dr. Minirth could help.

Through Bill's connection, Dr. Minirth agreed to see me. The problem was that I had nowhere to stay in Dallas. Remarkably, Bill's wife, Julie, had been saying for weeks that she felt God telling her, "Someone was supposed to come live with us." When Edward called about my situation, they realized I was that person. Despite having a fourteen-month-old baby and a tiny house, they invited me to stay with them. They didn't even have an extra bed, but the next day, Julie's friend inexplicably offered them a single bed she was about to throw out.

My parents surprisingly agreed to the plan. The next day, I checked out and went back to Dallas. Little did I know, my new life was truly about to begin.

PRAYER

Father, thank You for being the God who sees me in my darkest moments. When I feel stuck or hopeless, remind me of stories like this one where You orchestrated every detail perfectly. Open my eyes to see the people You've placed around me who can help and give me wisdom to know when to step in and be that person for someone else. Thank You that You're still in the business of working miracles through ordinary people and everyday phone calls. In Jesus' name. Amen.

24

Finding Community in the Wilderness

Remember how the LORD your God led you all the way in the wilderness these forty years, to humble and test you in order to know what was in your heart, whether or not you would keep his commands. —Deuteronomy 8:2

What does your spiritual community look like right now—the people who walk alongside you through the hard places?

I moved in with Bill and Julie. Bill took me to seminary classes with him. Most days, I would be at home with Julie and their toddler, Billy, and she would, day by day, principle by principle, teach me about God. I was getting a spiritual education, like I lived in my own residential seminary. But what I did not know was that as I was learning about God and how He heals our lives, He was doing it at the same time.

Bill and Julie sent me to see Dr. Minirth for my sessions, then they helped me process through what was taking place.

Bill also put a small group together for me: Edward, our good friend Fred, and a couple of other guys. We went deep into our lives, praying for each other, processing girlfriend pain and drama, sharing our fears for our futures, confessing our sins, and sometimes crying together about painful issues. We loved, supported, and healed one another in that small community that Bill and Julie had stewarded.

This time was my season of being led through the wilderness. When I look back, I can now say what Moses said: God brought me out with a mighty hand, performed miracles, and gave me a land (a life) that I could never have found on my own. And He has taught me His "ways," and as I have learned, they have transformed my entire life.

Where might God be inviting you into this kind of healing community today—either as someone who needs support or as someone who can offer it to others?

PRAYER

Father, sometimes I want You to just instantly fix everything that's broken in my life. But I'm reminded that You often work gradually. Help me trust Your timing and Your ways. Thank You for the people You've placed in my life to go through the wilderness with me. Give me patience with the process, and help me recognize the small miracles You're working, even in my wilderness. In Jesus' name. Amen.

25

When You Have Hidden Wounds, He Has Deeper Healing

Is anyone among you in trouble? Let them pray. Is anyone happy? Let them sing songs of praise. Is anyone among you sick? Let them call the elders of the church to pray over them and anoint them with oil in the name of the Lord. And the prayer offered in faith will make the sick person well; the Lord will raise them up. If they have sinned, they will be forgiven. Therefore confess your sins to each other and pray for each other so that you may be healed.

—James 5:13–16

Is it possible painful experiences from your past might still be affecting how you respond to challenges today?

As Christmas approached that year, Bill and Julie and I were watching *A Christmas Carol.* When Tiny Tim entered the scene on his crutches, I began to hyperventilate. I began to shake and tremble. Then, I began to have flashbacks of my childhood illness and of being that crippled kid . . . images of hospitals, people in white coats, loud X-ray machines, needles . . . It was like a whirling collage of terrifying pictures cascading through my head. I began to sob. Bill and Julie surrounded me and just held me until I could talk about what was happening.

What I did not understand at the time was that I was having PTSD symptoms from the physical pain and trauma that was done in those two years beginning around my fourth birthday. The illness that God had rescued me from through Dr. Sherman had been physically healed, but it had been lurking in my soul and psyche for all those years. I later understood that part of my breakdown in losing my ability to play golf was a big trigger that had sent me whirling into the pits of all the darkness that lay beneath. I was not just depressed over not being able to play competitive golf. I was reliving what had never healed underneath it all. The current loss was unearthing my buried childhood trauma and losses.

There were several other losses from my childhood and some physical abuse, which I began to process as well that year.

I had wanted God to "heal" me in an immediate flash of supernatural power—I had wanted Him to do that from the first day I turned to Him in that little chapel. He didn't, so I thought He wasn't going to. I had to learn to walk in faith and cope as best I could. I was learning to lean on Him for strength and was grateful to God for what I had seen Him do, but I was disappointed that He was not healing me. But the reality was that He was healing me at a much deeper level than I had been wanting. He was taking me through a deeper healing of my soul in these healing relationships. He was repairing me from the ground up.

Bill and Julie, Dr. Minirth, and my close spiritual community were supporting me, doing surgery in my soul as they made me process what was surfacing in therapy. They confronted me lovingly on unhealthy patterns in my life. They dug around in my soul, making me confess crummy attitudes, unforgiveness, and my performance orientation to prove myself. This was a tough treatment team.

I think we all need that. *You* need that.

PRAYER

Father, there are wounds in my life that I've tried to ignore or bury. Some are so old I barely remember them, but they still affect me today. Thank You that You see every hurt, every memory, every fear. Please guide me to the right people who can help me process these wounds. Give me patience with the journey and help me trust that You're working, even when I can't see it. In Jesus' name. Amen.

26

Breaking Free from Your False Self

You were taught, with regard to your former way of life, to put off your old self, which is being corrupted by its deceitful desires; to be made new in the attitude of your minds; and to put on the new self, created to be like God in true righteousness and holiness. Therefore each of you must put off falsehood and speak truthfully to your neighbor, for we are all members of one body.

—Ephesians 4:22–25

What masks do you wear to hide the parts of yourself that feel too vulnerable to show others?

I was learning the psychological, and biblical, construct of the "true self" and the "false self." I had built a false self that I began to show the outside world when I crawled out of that wheelchair and was going to prove I was not an inferior, crippled child. I was going to be an athlete. Every sport I could play, accomplishing state championships and regional championships in some, getting recruited to play NCAA golf. I was not cripple anymore . . . my false self had done its job. It kept the crippled child hidden, buried where no one would know. Or so I thought.

What psychology and later the Bible taught me was that a false self, which covers up who we really are, is a house built on sand. It will ultimately crash, and I was finding that to be more than true. Jesus called it being a "hypocrite," a term that literally meant "actor." One would go to the theater to see the "hypocrites" perform. The apostle Paul said the same thing, that we should "put off falsehood" (Eph. 4:25). My false self had cracked, and it was all coming to the surface, the truth that I was running from, long since forgotten. But PTSD does not lie, and trophies won't hide it. God was using my friends to tell me, "Give it up. Be true to yourself, God, and others."

Support, grief, uncovering things, processing pain, healing brokenheartedness, strengthening, modeling, risk-taking, weeping together, confession, forgiveness, repentance, changing thinking patterns, life examination and moral inventories, prayer, building new skills, and many more. They were all happening, and I had no clue. I was just "waiting for God to heal me." And since I was not able to "perform" and hide anymore, I was on the surgery table with no other choice. The false self had been dismantled.

Consider what your own false self might look like—the image you project to convince others (and maybe yourself) that you're strong, successful, or have it all together and . . . how might God be dismantling it?

PRAYER

God, I recognize now how much energy I've spent maintaining a false self, trying to prove I'm strong enough, good enough, perfect enough. Today, I choose to lay down that burden. I know it won't be easy—this performance has become so familiar. But I trust You to guide me through the dismantling process, to hold me as I grieve, and to show me who You created me to be. Help me embrace Your truth about my identity, even when it feels scary. In Jesus' name. Amen.

27

When Healing Doesn't Look Like You Expected

From him the whole body, joined and held together by every supporting ligament, grows and heals itself up in love, as each part does its work. —Ephesians 4:16

How often have you missed recognizing God's work in your life because it didn't come packaged the way you expected?

About a year later after my time with Bill and Julie, I was feeling pretty good. I had reentered college life and enrolled at SMU to continue there for my last two years. I was living in an apartment with Edward and another friend, had a new direction in life, a great spiritual community, had reconnected with my fraternity buddies, was dating again, and was feeling good about life. I had hope and a future.

I woke up one morning and was aware of something pretty startling . . . it had not really hit me in full force until that moment: *I am not depressed anymore.*

Perhaps there's an area in your life right now where you're waiting for God to act dramatically, while He's already working through the people around you.

It was true. I wasn't depressed. I felt pretty good. As I lay there letting that awareness sink in, thinking of all of the good things in my life at that point, I was so full and grateful to be this alive again. I was thanking God for all the people and direction I had now in my life. Then I had a thought: But I wish God had healed me.

I was disappointed that the God I had found had not healed me. I had not gotten "zapped" with a supernatural healing, making my depression go away. I lay there for a bit, kind of bummed that He had not done it.

Then a verse hit me, and I read it again, with that thought in mind: "From him the whole body, joined and held together by every supporting ligament, grows and heals itself up in love, as each part does its work" (Eph. 4:16).

Wait . . . "From Him"? From Jesus? "The whole body" (meaning His body of followers, His people)? As they are connected and each part does their work, we are healed? I was kind of speechless, embarrassed, and touched. I realized that was exactly what had happened to me. Jesus had connected me through supporting ligaments—His people—held me together and healed me as each part had done its work.

PRAYER

Father, I've been waiting for a dramatic breakthrough, but maybe You're already healing me through the people You've brought into my life. Thank You for Your body—the church—and for all the ways You work through others to bring comfort, wisdom, and healing. Help me lean into the community You've given me instead of trying to handle everything alone. Show me how to receive Your love through others and help me be part of Your healing work in someone else's life too. In Jesus' name. Amen.

28

God Can Bring Healing Through Others

Therefore encourage one another and build each other up, just as in fact you are doing. —1 Thessalonians 5:11

Who are the people God has strategically placed in your life as agents of healing and growth?

Julie, Bill, my doctor, my other friends who did all of those healing things were the "parts" of His body healing me just like the human body heals.

They cleaned out and flushed the infections in my soul, fought off the bacteria that were inside of me, strengthened my bones and put them back in place, took new material to the parts of me that were missing what I needed, and more. I realized it: God *did* heal me.

But He hadn't done it through a zapping. He had done it through a phone call that started the process and invited me out of my Egypt, putting me in the initial group that explained Jesus to me; brought person after person to answer my questions and Bible dilemmas; led me to the need for professional help; sent Edward to rescue me from my hospital prison; provided the doctor who knew what I needed; supernaturally spoke to the perfect young couple to take me into their home; provided them with the knowledge and skills to love me back into health; started breaking my PTSD down; placed me in a healing community and more.

I had to face the facts: God did heal me. And as He did it, I did not really even see all of what He was doing, because of my pain.

Take a moment to consider the "parts of His body" that God might be using in your life right now—people offering exactly what you need, perhaps in ways you haven't fully recognized.

PRAYER

Father, thank You for all the people You've strategically placed in my life—even the ones I haven't recognized as Your gifts yet. When I feel alone or stuck, remind me that You're actively working through the people around me. Help me trust the process, even when I can't see the full picture. Give me the courage to reach out and accept help from those You've sent to walk alongside me. In Jesus' name. Amen.

29

When God Redirects Your Path

I will instruct you and teach you in the way you should go; I will counsel you with my loving eye on you. —Psalms 32:8

What if the interruption to your plans is actually an invitation to something better than you had imagined?

Facing the next year, the darkness had gone, and I was at a place to begin contemplating *What now?* I was an accounting and finance major, but slowly realizing that it was not grabbing me. I had always done my schoolwork, and loved business, but the subject matter seemed more laborious than engaging. Plus, my first job in the financial world, working at the bank the summer before, had ended in me getting fired.

What I was noticing, though, was literally all of my free time was spent voraciously reading books about theology and my newest passion, psychology. I had gotten interested in it along the way trying to read my way out of my pain. Books that integrated spiritual growth and psychology held my interest especially. I devoured them.

Where in your life right now might God be stirring a new interest or passion that doesn't fit your original plan but feels surprisingly right?

In hang time with my friends, and with Bill and Julie and my group, when we were discussing the dynamics of our lives, my mind was kicking into gear in a way I had never felt before. I was seeing things that I had never noticed before, figuring out dilemmas and the issues that people were dealing with. I had empathy for people's pain, after what I had experienced. And I seemed to come alive inside when talking to people about their lives.

Person after person started saying things like, "You seem to see things in these discussions that others don't see. And you also seem to be able to relate the Bible to all of it in ways that others don't, too. Have you ever thought about becoming a psychologist?" Dr. Minirth began to ask me the same thing, saying that he saw an aptitude in me. One day, he just said point-blank, "I think you should either go to medical school and become a psychiatrist or get a PhD in clinical psychology."

I began to pray as sign after sign just kept appearing. And then, I felt as if God was saying "Go." Finally, I said, "Okay, God. I think You are calling me into this field. I surrender."

Lord, sometimes I wonder if I'm on the right track. Open my eyes to see the gifts You've given me—the ones others might notice before I do. Help me be brave enough to follow where You're leading, even if it means changing direction. Thank You for promising to guide me with Your loving eye. I trust You'll show me the way. In Jesus' name. Amen.

30

When God's Detour Becomes Your Destiny

A man's heart plans his way, but the LORD directs his steps.

—Proverbs 16:9 NKJV

Have you ever resisted a God-led change of direction because it seemed too difficult, too expensive, or too time-consuming?

God seemed to be changing my path, and I was scared. I had two years of a business major behind me and was obviously way behind in amassing the prerequisites that would be required for a graduate school PhD program. And then there was the reality of biting off five years of graduate school after college, an internship, plus another two years of supervised practice. I would not be legit for another seven-plus years of training. But I felt like God was saying "Go, and trust Me." I had to do it.

What step of faith might God be asking you to take today—one that requires trust because the logistics don't make sense on paper?

So, in faith, I changed my major to psych and enrolled in summer school to begin catching up with all of the prerequisites. A lot of work . . . but I loved it. I was alive. It felt like it was me. My heart loved this path, but it took God to begin to direct my steps. And He did.

Over the next two years, person after person appeared out of nowhere and began to mentor me and offer me great opportunities for real-world experience. I had doors open to get pretty advanced training. I was fortunate to have so many mentors take an interest in me and teach me so much. By the time I graduated from college, I had almost as much training in as many modalities as a third-year graduate student. And none of this was because I was very special or smarter than others in any way . . . it was all God opening doors to lead me in the path He wanted me to go. He was "directing my steps."

PRAYER

Lord, when I hear You calling me toward something new, the practical side of me keeps listing all the reasons it won't work. Help me trust that if You're calling me to something, You'll provide what I need to get there. Give me courage to take the first step. Thank You for directing my steps, even when they lead somewhere unexpected. In Jesus' name. Amen.

31

When God Establishes Your Plans

Commit to the LORD whatever you do, and he will establish your plans. The LORD works out everything to its proper end.

—Proverbs 16:3–4

When have you found yourself facing a transition, unsure of which direction to take next?

By the end of college, I wanted to confirm the calling, so I decided to take a gap year to work in a psychiatric hospital to see what this was really all about. Did I truly want to do this?

I prayed and searched. Then God intervened. Someone suggested I try to get a job as a psychiatric aide at the hospital where Dr. Minirth practiced. I didn't think I had a chance, but Minirth found out I was applying, and a few days later, the head nurse called to say they wanted to hire me.

The pay was minimum wage but I decided I could deal with a year of poverty to get the experience.

I went to work at the hospital, and it became clear God had brought me there. The doctors began to bring me into their groups, and have me follow their patients through the days, helping implement treatment plans, and I worked closely with the nursing staff on the unit. The experience I was gaining was almost like being a psychiatric resident.

As the months of my gap year were passing by, they began to inquire about my graduate school plans. They called me in and told me they wanted me to get my training somewhere close to Dallas, because they wanted me to work for them and become a partner in their practice! They also said they could help pay for school, and when I got through the master's level, I could begin seeing patients. My future seemed to be secure and opening up before my eyes.

PRAYER

Lord, I often find myself at a crossroads, trying to figure out my next steps. Sometimes I feel like I should have it all figured out, but I don't. Help me to trust that when I commit my plans to You, You will guide me—even if the path looks different from what I expected. Give me courage to take those first steps of faith. In Jesus' name. Amen.

32

Trust and Obey

Trust in the LORD with all your heart and lean not on your own understanding; in all your ways submit to him, and he will make your paths straight. —Proverbs 3:5–6

When was the last time you felt an unexpected, almost unexplainable certainty about a decision that seemed to go against logic?

I had an amazing offer to go to school in Dallas and work for Dr. Minirth. I was set.

But I had also sent an application to Biola University in Los Angeles, just because some of the best writing and research in the integration of psychology and theology was coming out of that school. It was known for the best clinical training in the country in that niche. I had applied for fun, knowing there was no way on God's green earth I was going to move to California. It was a little like a kid applying to Harvard just to see if he could get in.

Then I got a letter from Biola saying I had gotten past the first stage of applications and was granted an interview. They would send someone to Dallas to conduct interviews for applicants from that area of the country and sent me an appointment time. I thought, *No reason to go to this, but what the heck, why not just do it for grins and to learn something?*

The interview went well, and I liked the guy. We connected in a lot of ways about how we viewed psychology and faith. But I had no thoughts of anything past just the interview.

And then, it happened.

Something came over me . . . It was not like I changed my mind . . . it was like my mind was changed from the outside. It was a shift that I was almost an observer to. It was like my "being" was morphed into a certain awareness and almost command: I was going to Los Angeles.

I have no idea how God did that, but I know it was Him. I walked out knowing I was supposed to go to California for my training.

As Proverbs 16:9 said, "the LORD directs his steps" (NKJV). I was being directed.

I told Dr. Minirth and his partners that I was leaving, packed up my little Toyota with all my earthly belongings, no money to speak of, and took off. I was reminded of Abraham, whom God called out of His land to the Promised Land. In

Hebrews 11:8–10, the author mentions that Abraham left Ur, not knowing where he was going, but he knew he was going to a city whose architect was God. I had no idea what I was doing, or what I was headed for, other than the architect of it all was God. All I could do was "trust." As the old hymn says, "Trust and obey, for there is no other way."

So, off to LA. And it was a big step of trust.

But I had an awareness of something that had grown in me: God will make a way. He knew where He was taking me all the while. So, as I drove, scared in a lot of ways, I also felt a growing sense of anticipation of what He was going to do.

PRAYER

Lord, there are moments when Your direction catches me completely off guard. You're inviting me to step away from my comfortable plans into something unknown. You've proven faithful before and I know You are faithful still. Like Abraham, help me step out in faith even when I can't see the whole path ahead. Give me courage to trust Your leading, even when it means letting go of what feels secure. In Jesus' name. Amen.

33

When God Writes Your Story

"For I know the plans I have for you," declares the LORD, "plans to prosper you and not to harm you, plans to give you hope and a future." —Jeremiah 29:11

Looking back, what chapters of your life story have seemed random or disconnected, but later revealed themselves as part of a greater purpose?

As I look back, I can see the collection of wildly creative and unexpected miracles God brought to bring me to the time when I had gotten broken, to healing my depression, to finding my life's calling as a psychologist. As you reflect on your own journey, where can you see God's fingerprints on events that once appeared coincidental or even painful?

He answered my prayer that first desperate day back in college in so many profound and life-changing ways that I was unable to recognize at the time as being the miraculous supernatural interventions that they were.

God is an active worker of miracles, both in the mundane corners of our lives and in big, bold ways that literally move mountains. Some of what's happened in my life may seem "circumstantial," but the impossible odds and ways they developed, which were totally outside of my orchestrating, is miraculous to me.

While I am sharing with you some of the great things He has done for me, remember all the good things God has brought about were also riddled with a lot of pain, struggle, defeat, and failure. Don't think a journey with God, like mine, is all a bed of roses.

Like the man He healed who had been blind from birth, all I can tell you is that I was a mess, and He has done a lot to make it better. And the message to you from me is this: He wants to be in and work miracles in your life too. Whether you are stuck like I was, or doing "great," He has a plan for you that is better than you will ever know.

PRAYER

Father, I'm grateful that You see the bigger picture when I can only see my current struggles. Thank You for being active in every detail of my life, even when I don't recognize Your hand at work. When I feel broken or lost, remind me that You're still writing my story. Help me trust Your timing and Your plans, knowing that You're working everything together for good. In Jesus' name. Amen.

34

Finding God in the Contradictions

"I have told you these things, so that in me you may have peace. In this world you will have trouble. But take heart! I have overcome the world." —John 16:33

Do you ever struggle to make sense of how blessings and suffering so often seem to coexist?

The Bible depicts a life that can seem contradictory and confusing. Yet one of the things that helps me know the Bible is true is that it talks about life the way it really is. It depicts life exactly as we see it. Think about your own journey with God—how have you experienced both His promises of blessing and the reality of difficulties, sometimes simultaneously?

First the Bible says God will be with us, bless us in various ways, protect us, lead us, and guide us. And at the same time, on the same pages, it says horrible things might happen to us as well. Death, loss, disease, betrayal, poverty. It is such a contradictory message. But it is exactly true to the life we see, even after we begin to follow Him.

I always say God has a marketing issue. Brands try to paint a totally positive picture of what they are selling. In God's marketing, He does promise us a lot of good stuff... Jesus said to follow Him in order to have an "abundant" life. But He also promised us suffering, and even extra suffering if we follow Him. Not exactly a great marketing approach: "Buy this product, and you will get to carry your cross daily! Buy a life with Me and it will cost you big time."

The only one who ever did it perfectly in God's storyline got crucified.

That is what makes suffering with God different from suffering without Him—when we suffer with Him, we do not suffer alone; He is with us.

PRAYER

God, sometimes life feels like a contradiction. One day I'm on the mountaintop, the next in the valley. Help me trust You when things don't make sense, remembering You promised both blessings and challenges. Thank You for being honest with me about what following You means. Most of all, thank You for staying close in both the good and hard times. In Jesus' name. Amen.

35

When a Past Failure Holds You Hostage

Moses said to the LORD, "Pardon your servant, Lord. I have never been eloquent, neither in the past nor since you have spoken to your servant. I am slow of speech and tongue." —Exodus 4:10

Is there a moment of failure or humiliation from your past that still affects how you see yourself or what you're willing to try?

It was a horrible day that limited my life for years after. In seventh or eighth grade, during oral book reports—something I usually enjoyed—I got flustered a third of the way through. I began stammering and couldn't recover. The teacher said, "Just sit down. This is terrible." She berated me, "You'll never be successful if you can't do public speaking. And forget being a lawyer, because lawyers have to talk in front of people." Maybe you have your own version of that English class moment—an experience where someone's words or your own perceived failure created a limitation you've accepted as permanent.

Devastated and ashamed, I slithered into my seat. From there, public speaking became impossible. I could handle small groups at a table, but anything larger and I literally couldn't speak. Through high school and college, I avoided it completely. My parents sent me to a counselor, but it didn't help. I nearly flunked twelfth-grade English over an oral report requirement, willing to lose my college golf recruitment rather than speak.

In my midtwenties, I had built a practice and developed models for psychological and leadership growth, and I was constantly asked to speak for organizations and businesses. I always refused, saying, "No, that's just not something I do." I stuck to my private clinical and consulting practice. Small meetings were fine, but nothing larger.

Then one day at the gym, heading to the showers, this big naked guy walked up to me. He was huge—he had played NFL football for the LA Rams. I wondered what he wanted when he looked at me and asked, "Are you a Christian?"

That seemed weird . . . big naked guy randomly walking up to me asking if I am a Christian.

I'll tell you the rest of that story . . . tomorrow.

PRAYER

Father, You know that moment in my life. The one that still makes me cringe. The one I've let define what's possible for me. I choose to hand You that memory, that shame, that limitation. I'm tired of letting one failure write my story. Like You did with Moses, show me how much bigger Your plans are than my past. In Jesus' name. Amen.

36

Your Past Doesn't Determine Your Future

"I will repay you for the years the locusts have eaten—the great locust and the young locust, the other locusts and the locust swarm—my great army that I sent among you. You will have plenty to eat, until you are full,and you will praise the name of the LORD your God, who has worked wonders for you; never again will my people be shamed." —Joel 2:25–26

Would you let me guess something about you? I bet you have accepted limitations about yourself, and that God is challenging you to reconsider it. That was true in my life.

Remember the big naked guy randomly walked up to me asking if I was a Christian?

"Uh . . . yeah," I answered.

"Well, God just told me to tell you something." He explained he was a pastor at the Newport Vineyard Church, so I agreed to talk to him.

We went to a restaurant, and he said: "God said that when you were a kid, something bad happened to you that has made you afraid to speak in front of people ever since. But He wants you to begin speaking for Him, and He is going to open some doors. You are to walk through them."

I was stunned. In high school, I had prayed for God to help with this problem, and He never did. But now, it seemed He was stepping up. That naked guy didn't know me or anything about my problem.

The next week, I got two calls to speak to public groups. The first was to fifty Presbyterian pastors. That would have been far more than I could normally handle, but I felt like I had no choice. I asked a friend who's a speech therapist to come with me for support. I stumbled through it, but at least I got through that first test without passing out.

From there, more "doors" mysteriously appeared. I was petrified each time, but gradually got more comfortable. It took about a year to feel at ease. Then, I was offered a radio show.

That was decades ago . . . since then I have spoken thousands of times. Now, I actually enjoy it. As a psychologist, I believe the slow healing came through natural processes. But there's no doubt the impetus to get me into that process was supernatural. How else can you explain it?

Where might God be calling *you* to step through a door that your past experiences have convinced you to keep closed?

PRAYER

Father, there are things in my past that still affect me today—fears and hurts that feel like they define who I am and what I can do. But You are bigger than my past and bigger than my fears. When You open doors for me, help me remember this story and trust that Your plan is good, even when it feels overwhelming. Thank You for being patient with my process of healing and growth. In Jesus' name. Amen.

37

Following God's Guidance

For this God is our God for ever and ever; he will be our guide even to the end. —Psalms 48:14

Have you ever felt an unexplainable prompting to do something that seemed illogical but turned out to be exactly what was needed?

It was the end of the day when my pager went off. I called my answering service, and they patched me through to a woman calling from a phone booth. She was a new patient I had seen for only a couple of weeks but was pretty depressed. I had discussed with her the possibility of hospitalization if the depression got worse. She had resisted.

"Hey," I said. "What's happening?"

"Nothing," she said in a voice that did not sound good. "But I wanted to call you and thank you for trying to help me. I know you want to . . . but I just can't do this. I just can't. So, thank you anyway."

And she hung up.

I knew what that meant. She had promised to call me if she felt suicidal, but something had changed. She was going to do it.

I had no idea where she was. This was before cell phones. I called her home, but no one was there. I was totally in the dark, and very scared.

When I feel scared, I pray. I asked God to keep her safe. Then I felt a prompting to get in my car and look for her. It made no sense—Southern California is a big place. But I followed the urge.

That's not easy, is it? Think about the times when you've dismissed a nudge or prompting as impractical or irrational—might some of those have been divine guidance you missed?

I felt led to drive to South Coast Plaza, a massive shopping center with over 250 stores and miles of parking lots. Even if she was there, how would I find her? But at each turn, I felt guided where to go next.

I turned down a row of cars and there it was: her car. I got out, and found her lying in the back seat, detached, with pills ready to take them.

She fully recovered after therapy. Years later, she had three children and a great marriage. The chances of finding her car right in time apart from God? In my mind, zero.

PRAYER

Father, I often doubt those quiet nudges You send my way. Sometimes Your promptings seem illogical, and I hesitate to follow. Help me recognize Your voice more clearly and give me the courage to act when You lead. Thank You that You're already working in situations where I feel helpless. Teach me to trust You even when the path forward seems impossible. Guide my steps today, Lord, just as You guided this doctor to save a precious life. In Jesus' name. Amen.

38

Trusting God When Your Obedience Attracts Attacks

"No weapon forged against you will prevail, and you will refute every tongue that accuses you. This is the heritage of the servants of the LORD, and this is their vindication from me," declares the LORD. —Isaiah 54:17

Have you ever faced opposition or criticism for doing what you believed was right, where following God's leading attracted resistance rather than applause?

One example where I followed God into a promise, experienced pain, and found Him present was when I began our psychiatric hospital company. After seeking God's direction while in private practice, I committed to praying every Thursday evening with a friend about our next steps. After a year, it became clear God was calling me to begin a faith-based hospital. With Dr. John Townsend, we built treatment centers with an incredible team that was healing and changing lives.

Besides start-up difficulties, I discovered that dealing with gnarly family situations on a large scale invited trouble. Hospital work involved abuse cases and extended family conflict that was staggering. When you help someone escape abuse, sometimes the abusers come after those who helped. Sometimes churches didn't like it either, thinking we were turning people away from God. They wrote articles about how bad our teachings were.

One church group even broke into the hospital through the ER at night in special ops clothing to "rescue" a church member who had admitted herself for depression. In their minds, they had lost control of her to us—the "secular humanists."

During this challenging time, I felt victimized and distressed over the threats. One night after praying about it, someone approached me saying he had had a vision. He said God showed him a wall of fire surrounding my "house"—which wasn't really a house but my place of work—with angels protecting it specifically from attacking family members. He drew what he had seen, showing the hospital being shielded by God.

We continued to be protected, with no threats materializing into anything serious. Even when a man fresh from prison called threatening to kill Dr. Townsend, police arrested him before anything happened. It was another example of how

God is with us, even when things are hard, and how a supernatural vision from a stranger brought security amid the chaos.

PRAYER

God, sometimes following You feels scary. When I step out in obedience, I know I might face opposition. Help me remember that wall of fire You build around Your people. Thank You that You don't just call me to difficult things and leave me alone—You stay right there with me. Give me courage to keep following You, even when it's hard. Help me trust that You'll protect me, and give me the boldness to keep moving forward, knowing You're my protector. In Jesus' name. Amen.

39

Finding God's Purpose in Unexpected Friendships

Be wise in the way you act toward outsiders; make the most of every opportunity. Let your conversation be always full of grace, seasoned with salt, so that you may know how to answer everyone.

—Colossians 4:5–6

Are there unexpected people God has placed in your life who you may have overlooked? I think that happens to all of us.

My wife, Tori, and I love boats. For years, we had one anchored in Newport Harbor. One morning, we woke up on our boat to find an interesting beautiful older boat had pulled into the slip next to us during the night. It was a beautiful classic old trawler that had just returned from Hawaii.

I was admiring it when the owners came out on deck, and we started talking. While having dinner one night, they shared the real reason they were there.

Nick had pancreatic cancer. He was a successful tech entrepreneur who had cashed out of his company at fifty, and he and Kaitlin had just begun their adventure of traveling the world when he got the news. It did not look good; his cancer had a very low survival rate. They had come to Orange County to see a specialist and were going to live on their boat.

As weeks passed, Nick and I became good friends. We shared a passion for boats, business, and red wine. He was funny. I enjoyed hearing his business story.

In the process, I had shared my story too, and he knew about my faith-based hospitals and books on faith and psychology. One day, he opened up.

"So, I need to talk to you about something," he said. "About God."

He explained that he had converted to Judaism from Presbyterian beliefs because the Trinity seemed like three Gods to him. "But the problem is that I do not hear of a lot of Jews praying or believing in healing . . . only the Christians do. And I know you are one, and I wanted you to pray for me," he said. "I need healing."

I wonder who God has put in your life who you could show His love to or offer to pray for?

"Of course," I assured Nick, "I would love to, and I also would love to hear more about your faith story."

So, I prayed for him and had others praying for him as well. I loved Nick . . . I didn't want him to die.

——PRAYER——

God, open my eyes to see the people You put in my path today. I confess I sometimes rush past opportunities to connect, thinking I'm too busy or it's just a casual encounter. Help me remember that You might have positioned me exactly where I am for someone else. Give me wisdom to build genuine friendships, patience to earn trust, and courage to share my faith when the moment comes. In Jesus' name. Amen.

40

When Religion Pushes People Away, Love Brings Them Home

"All those the Father gives me will come to me, and whoever comes to me I will never drive away. . . . For my Father's will is that everyone who looks to the Son and believes in him shall have eternal life, and I will raise them up at the last day." —JOHN 6:37, 40

We need to share our faith with people who don't believe, but have you ever thought about how our *approach* to sharing faith can either draw people closer to God or push them further away?

Yesterday I told you about Kaitlin and Nick, our neighbors when we were living on a boat. Nick had cancer and Kaitlin, a believer in Jesus, pulled me aside after dinner one night and asked me to talk to him about faith, wanting assurance he would be in heaven. Nick had left Christianity due to bad church experiences and converted to Judaism. Soon after we began these talks, Nick's health declined severely.

One Saturday morning, Kaitlin called: "You have to come down to the boat . . . Nick is going to die today." When Tori and I arrived, I went to see him in the master stateroom. He managed a tiny smile.

I said, "Nick, can I talk to you about God for a little?"

He nodded eagerly.

I explained that I understood his negative church experiences, then continued: "Remember when you were learning about the Passover? Remember how there was a lamb to be sacrificed, and the blood of the lamb was put on the doorpost? And then the angel of death would 'pass over' that house?"

He nodded.

"Jesus is that Passover Lamb, the Messiah who was prophesied. He was sacrificed to pay the death penalty for all of us. He lived a perfect life and was the only one who could pay for our imperfection. His resurrection proved His claims. Would you like to receive Him as your Passover Lamb now?"

Nick looked up and nodded yes.

I led him in a simple prayer to accept Jesus. Tears began streaming down his face. His expression changed—he was at peace with God. I kissed his forehead and said, "It's okay now, Nick. I know you need rest."

He squeezed my hand, still teary, and I left. When I walked upstairs, Kaitlin looked at me, and I nodded yes. She knew what that meant and ran down to the stateroom.

Who in your life might need someone to meet them where they are spiritually, with acceptance rather than judgment, as they navigate their own journey toward God?

PRAYER

Father, my heart breaks when I think about people who've been pushed away from You. Help me be more like Jesus—someone who draws people in rather than pushes them away. When I meet people who are skeptical of faith because of past wounds, give me wisdom to listen well and speak Your truth with gentleness. Show me how to help them see past the human mess to Your perfect love. In Jesus' name. Amen.

41

Finding God's Comfort at Death's Door

"My sheep listen to my voice; I know them, and they follow me. I give them eternal life, and they shall never perish; no one will snatch them out of my hand." —John 10:27–28

Have you ever witnessed something so profound it changed how you understand the boundary between heaven and earth? I have.

After sharing the gospel with Nick, I told Tori what happened. Then we heard a painful scream and ran downstairs to find Kaitlin convulsively sobbing over Nick's body. He was gone. We helped her upstairs where she collapsed, sobbing. Months of pain were breaking loose as she fell into the grief she had carried.

Tori knelt over her as she sobbed on her knees. I looked up across the salon where Tori was kneeling over Kaitlin, and standing next to them was Jesus, and Nick. I cannot fully describe how I saw them—it wasn't like seeing people with my physical eyes. They were almost translucent, as if in another dimension. I saw them somehow in my spirit, even though I perceived them visually across the room.

They stood over Kaitlin as she wailed, just watching her, being with her. Then they instantly flew up and left through the ceiling and wall into the sky. Gone in an instant.

Later, Kaitlin told us that after Nick had connected with Jesus, she had told him, "I know what happened with Henry. It's okay now. You don't have to hold on anymore. You can go."

She said he looked into her eyes and nodded. Then suddenly, his face filled with awareness and amazement. His eyes opened wide as he looked upward at something that had caught his full attention. His face lit up with what she described as a "total realization." Then he was gone.

I know he saw Jesus, his newly found Jewish Messiah, coming to take him home.

In those sacred moments between life and death, perhaps you too have sensed something beyond what eyes can see—a comfort that transcends explanation.

PRAYER

Lord, there are moments when the veil between heaven and earth feels paper-thin, and other times when You seem a million miles away. Help me remember You are always near, even when I can't sense Your Presence. Thank You for walking through the valley of death with us. In Jesus' name. Amen.

42

When God Whispers Through Others

The LORD said, "Go out and stand on the mountain in the presence of the LORD, for the LORD is about to pass by." Then a great and powerful wind tore the mountains apart and shattered the rocks before the LORD, but the LORD was not in the wind. After the wind there was an earthquake, but the LORD was not in the earthquake. After the earthquake came a fire, but the LORD was not in the fire. And after the fire came a gentle whisper.

—1 Kings 19:11–12

When was the last time someone's seemingly random suggestion completely changed your direction?

Most people didn't marry their prom date. We can all probably relate to some period of traveling through and negotiating the world of "dating." It can be a lot of fun and/or a fair amount of brain damage.

I was in my midtwenties and had dated a lot of really great women. I could see that I had a pattern. There were women who were wonderful people, who I liked, was attracted to, and had good relationships with. Until . . . for some reason, I would slowly begin to feel depressed. Interest would wane, and I would feel like it is just not the right relationship. So, I would leave.

As part of psychology training, we were required to have therapy. After one more failed relationship, my therapist said, "I think you need to see a woman therapist for this issue. There is something I am not getting to that you need to work through."

"But Phil . . . you are the best. Why can't you do it?" I asked.

And this I think was the "God" moment:

He said, "I don't know . . . it is just a feeling I get. You need a woman therapist."

Little did I know that God was about to change my life again.

He suggested Althea Horner, who had just moved from New York to LA. At the time, she was one of the most heralded names in psychodynamic therapy. She wrote the textbooks we had studied, and she lectured worldwide.

Consider the patterns in your own life that might need a fresh perspective—where might God be trying to speak to you through someone else's insight?

I called directory assistance and got her number. When I called, expecting gatekeepers, she answered directly. I told her I was a beginning psychologist looking for a new therapist. "Well, I just moved here and haven't really set up a practice yet . . . but this sounds interesting. Why don't you come in and let's talk about it," she said.

Of course, I went, and for some reason, she agreed to work with me.

PRAYER

Lord, sometimes I'm so busy looking for big signs that I miss Your gentle whispers through others. Help me to be attentive to the small nudges, the random suggestions, and the unexpected conversations that might be Your way of guiding me. Give me the courage to follow these leads, even when they seem unlikely or uncomfortable. Thank You for the people You place in my path who become Your voice of direction in my life. In Jesus' name. Amen.

43

When Your Therapist Becomes God's Divine Connection

You turned my wailing into dancing; you removed my sackcloth and clothed me with joy, that my heart may sing your praises and not be silent. LORD my God, I will praise you forever.

—Psalms 30:11–12

Has something ever happened that was so unlikely, so perfectly orchestrated, that you knew it couldn't possibly be coincidence?

I went through the early phases with my new therapist Althea. We talked about my dating history and all the usual stuff. Later, I developed a hernia and had to go in for surgery. As it approached, I began to have weird anxiety, almost panic-type feelings.

I told Althea. She asked about my hospital experiences, and I told her about my childhood illness, being in a wheelchair and braces, and how hard it was for me and my family. She asked how I got better, and I told her about a woman doctor who saved my leg from amputation and how she really saved my life. My whole world revolved around her for a couple of years. I really loved her.

Althea asked, “Do you still see her?”

“No,” I said.

“Why not? Seems like you would at least keep in touch after all of that.”

“She died.”

“Oh no . . . when? How?”

“She was murdered . . . right as I was finishing treatment with her.”

Althea’s face turned white. She leaned forward and said, “Her name was Mary Sherman.”

“Yes . . . how did you know that?” I asked.

“She was my best friend,” Althea said.

What happened from there brought the healing I needed. Althea brought in pictures of Dr. Sherman and told me stories about her. Through that, the grief over losing this powerful second mother began to come out.

As I worked through that grief, it became clear why I would get depressed and bail out of good relationships as they got closer. Getting close would activate the loss that still lived in my soul, and I would push away to avoid another loss.

Think about the unresolved losses in your own life—could some of your current patterns be connected to grief you haven't fully processed?

Althea helped me discover that loss, re-create Mary Sherman, and grieve her, which healed that dynamic in my life. It's why I was later able to marry Tori with no fear at all. We've been married twenty-eight years now, thanks to Althea and God's mysterious way of leading me to the one therapist who could have re-created Dr. Sherman for me.

PRAYER

Lord, sometimes the wounds I carry are so deep I don't even know they're there. Thank You for seeing what I can't and orchestrating healing in ways I could never imagine. Help me trust You with my unspoken grief and hidden fears. When I'm tempted to run from love or protect myself from pain, remind me that You are the ultimate Healer who can transform my deepest hurts into pathways for connection. In Jesus' name. Amen.

44

When You Have to Wait

Wait for the LORD; be strong and take heart and wait for the LORD. —Psalms 27:14

What are you waiting for that tests your patience and challenges your trust in God's timing?

My dating years included a lot of drama, and some God moments along the way. He entered into the pain and healed me of what was holding me back. But I still had to find her . . . the one.

Right after a breakup with a particular woman I thought had real possibilities, I was really discouraged about ever finding the "right one." I was in my room, disappointed with God.

My dating life had developed a theme. There would be great girls with wonderful character and values, but the chemistry would be missing. Then there were women I really connected with chemistry-wise, but either spiritual depth or our values were not the same.

Perhaps you're facing your own version of this dilemma right now—wanting something good but finding that each option seems to be missing something essential.

I was talking to God about this problem in my room one night, and felt a very strong "go open your Bible" prompting. If you don't have a relationship with God, that might sound weird. But if you have for a long time, you know what it feels like.

I picked up my Bible and it "randomly" fell open to this verse: "'We are witnesses! May the Lord make this woman who is coming into your home like Rachel and Leah, from whom all the nation of Israel descended!'" (Ruth 4:11 NLT).

This really got me: She would be like Rachel and Leah. Both of them. Jacob had been very attracted to Rachel (the magic and chemistry), while Leah was the one who had the great character. Rachel and Leah represented the two kinds of women I kept finding, never able to find both in one person.

What I knew God was saying was that He was going to bring someone to me who would be everything I had longed for. Someone I would be in love with who also had all the values and depth I cared about.

I knew that He had spoken to me.

PRAYER

Father, sometimes I'm not very good at waiting. When things aren't happening on my timeline, I get restless and start doubting.

Help me learn to recognize Your voice, even in the quiet moments of disappointment. Thank You that You still speak to us today—through Your Word, through promptings, through the quiet moments. Give me courage to wait well and wisdom to hear clearly. In Jesus' name. Amen.

45

Trusting God's Perfect Timing

I wait for the LORD, my whole being waits, and in his word I put my hope. I wait for the Lord more than watchmen wait for the morning, more than watchmen wait for the morning. Israel, put your hope in the LORD, for with the LORD is unfailing love and with him is full redemption. —Psalms 130:5–7

How long have you been waiting for something you believe God has promised you? If it's been a long time, I understand.

I knew God had spoken to me through the verses in Ruth—a woman would be coming into my home. What I ignored in the passage is the seven years that Jacob had to wait.

Well, the years went on. Then, one night at a Christmas party, a friend brought a guest whom I started talking to and was very interested in. She was in her early twenties, which seemed too young for me in my early thirties, so I passed.

But I did not forget her. Roll the clock forward almost a year later, and I saw her at a party. Five months after that, I saw her again at a business dinner.

This time, something hit me. It felt like God was putting her there. I called a friend who prays for me and told him if it was from God, I wanted Him to arrange another "random" meeting as a sign.

Four months later, at a graduation ceremony, I met her mother, who said, "You know, Tori's in town. You should call her."

I called her and we went out, but the first date was horrible. She seemed distant and cool. I tried one more time, and after several rejected suggestions, she quickly agreed to a date just to get me off the phone.

On our second date, we had a great time. She was only planning to be in town for a two-week art institute, but she decided to stick around longer. Longer turned into longer, and here we still are, twenty-eight years later. My biggest gift from God.

PRAYER

Father, when it feels like nothing's happening, help me remember You're always at work. Give me wisdom to recognize Your hand in the "random" moments of my life, and courage to wait for Your best rather than settling for less. In Jesus' name. Amen.

46

When God Calls You Beyond Your Comfort Zone

"For my thoughts are not your thoughts, neither are your ways my ways," declares the LORD. "As the heavens are higher than the earth, so are my ways higher than your ways and my thoughts than your thoughts." —Isaiah 55:8–9

Have you ever been in that awkward place where you felt God calling you to step away from something that seemed perfectly good in order—you believe—to pursue something better?

It was "free agent" time in my publishing career, when you're not tied down and free to sign with anyone. After a season of meetings, we had reached a good agreement for several books that would give me a clear path for about five years. We had finalized negotiations and would be signing in a few days.

I was at home talking with Tori when my phone rang. It was a woman with whom I served on a board. I knew her, but not well, and she knew nothing about my work with publishers.

"Hey, Shelly. How are you?" I asked.

"I'm good," she said. "But I just had a vision about you. I saw you in a yard, talking to people, and there was a fence around all of you. And then the Lord said: 'You have been speaking to people in the yard, and I want to remove the fence so you can speak to people outside the yard.' And He says you're about to sign some contract about a book project, and if you sign it, it will keep you in that yard. So don't sign it."

The deal was with a Christian publisher. If the publisher is Christian, retailers often bury it in the religious section. The marketing would be mostly to the Christian world—the people in the yard. God was telling me He wanted me to talk to people outside the Christian world.

Where might God be asking you to leave your comfortable "yard" to reach people who would never enter your usual circles?

For about a year and a half, when I would pray, I would hear a voice say, "I am taking you out of the ministry." To me, "ministry" meant Christian audiences, which was most of what I did.

I hung up bummed. Everything had looked so good, but when God says "Go," you do it, and you leave security behind. So, I walked away from the deal.

PRAYER

God, I'll be honest—I like my comfort zone. But if You're calling me to something different, even if it doesn't make sense, give me the courage to say yes. Help me recognize Your voice when You speak, whether it's through prayer, other people, or that nudge in my spirit. And when You say "Go," give me the faith to take that first scary step. In Jesus' name. Amen.

47

When God Opens Unexpected Doors

And pray for us, too, that God may open a door for our message, so that we may proclaim the mystery of Christ. —Colossians 4:3

Have you ever walked away from something secure only to find God had something better waiting that you couldn't have anticipated?

When I told the publisher I was not going through with the contract he was dumbfounded. I have to admit it didn't make any sense, unless you were on the phone call where Shelly gave me the message from God, "Don't sign it."

Soon after, Time Life called with an offer to do a book with a national secular media campaign that would take the message way past the Christian audience. John Townsend and I wrote *God Will Make a Way*, and talking to people outside the yard had begun.

But there was more to come. God put me with an outside-the-yard publishing agent who wanted to do my first secular business book. I would be writing to businesses without the Christian language, which meant they could use the principles in their public companies. This step fulfilled the vision God gave me about talking to people "outside the yard."

We went to New York and published a leadership book that showed the principles I had been using with leaders but had no Bible verses in it. The *New York Times* reviewed the book (*Integrity*) and called it "the best book of the bunch." Had God not guided me, I would have missed so many great opportunities to work with people who don't hang out in that yard, for purposes that were His.

I wonder where in your life God might be asking you to trust His direction even when it doesn't make practical sense?

PRAYER

God, I confess I often want to play it safe in my Christian comfort zone. But maybe You're calling me to something bigger—to share Your truth in ways that connect with people who might never walk into a church. Give me creativity and courage to speak Your wisdom in ways that make sense to others. In Jesus' name. Amen.

48

How to Listen When God Has You Pray for Healing

LORD my God, I called to you for help, and you healed me.
—Psalms 30:2

When was the last time you had a persistent thought or impression that wouldn't go away?

I had landed in Phoenix and was checking into my hotel, getting ready to speak to Jewish rabbis who believe in Jesus as the Jewish Messiah. I walked into my hotel room to unpack, and it happened.

I saw a very clear internal vision in my head of a kneecap. I heard the word "kneecap" go through my head. It kept repeating: Kneecap. Kneecap. Kneecap.

I went down to the ballroom where the five hundred or so rabbis were gathered. During my talks over the next day, the word "kneecap" kept repeating in my head. At my final talk that evening, I knew I had to do something. So, at the end, I said to the audience: "I am not one of those preacher types who goes on TV and says things like this . . . but I feel like there is someone here who might have something going on with their kneecap and need prayer for it."

After praying, a tall Middle Eastern man approached me and said, "I am the one with the knee you were praying for. I have had an infection under my kneecap for a while and the doctors cannot figure it out, and the pain is unbearable at times. I was crying out to God silently to please help me. Then, you prayed . . . and when you did, I felt a bolt of electricity go through my entire body, and it was like my knee caught on fire.

"I am healed," he exclaimed. He then rolled up his pants leg, pulled off a knee brace, and threw it across the room.

I can safely call that one a miracle.

What might happen in or through you if you paid attention to those seemingly random impressions or thoughts that keep recurring, treating them as possible promptings from God?

PRAYER

God, sometimes I doubt those gentle nudges or repeated thoughts might be from You. Help me be brave enough to act on them, even when I feel uncertain. Give me courage to step out when You prompt me and help me trust that You can use even my stumbling attempts to bring healing to others. In Jesus' name. Amen.

49

Serving Others When You Feel Powerless

Carry each other's burdens, and in this way you will fulfill the law of Christ. —Galatians 6:2

Where do you find yourself carrying the weight of others' pain or struggles?

I love the practice of clinical psychology. More than that, though, I love being able to play a part in relieving someone's suffering. I just like helping people. And past the painful cases, I also really love seeing people just "get better," even if they are already a high performer, like a CEO or professional athlete who is already thriving but wants to go from "good to great." I love seeing people thrive . . . taking the next step and winning.

But it is not all roses. Psychologists suffer along with their patients. Some research has shown that practicing psychologists die sooner than those in other fields.

Most of the difficulty comes not from difficult patients but from seeing the suffering and hearing the evil that has been inflicted on some people. Sometimes I have left the session and vomited after hearing what happened to someone. Some people's abuse is unimaginable.

The other pain psychologists experience from time to time is, for me, the hardest: pure powerlessness. It is the feeling of *I just don't know what to do now to help. Nothing I am doing right now is making this better.*

You probably aren't a psychologist, but still you know the heaviness of witnessing suffering you can't fix. That is why, many times, I have been so grateful that I was not doing this alone. God was there and many times intervened.

PRAYER

Lord, sometimes the weight of others' pain feels too heavy to carry. When I encounter stories that break my heart or situations I can't fix, remind me that You're the true Healer. Thank You that I don't have to have all the answers—You do. Give me wisdom to know when to act and when to simply be present. Help me remember that while I'm called to serve, I'm not called to save. In Jesus' name. Amen.

50

Experiencing His Help When We're Helpless

"Arise, shine, for your light has come, and the glory of the LORD rises upon you. For darkness covers the earth and thick darkness is over the peoples, but the LORD rises upon you and his glory appears over you." —Isaiah 60:1–2

You reach the end of your resources and abilities. You have nowhere to turn but to God. It is a desperate, and a great, place to be.

I was treating a physician who suffered from severe PTSD from being raped as a little girl. It emerged in her early thirties, leading to depression and dissociative episodes. She was still able to work, as the dissociation only occurred when personally triggered—by violent TV shows, movies with hurt children, or family calls.

On this day in my office, she hit a memory that put her over the edge. She flipped into what seemed like a four-year-old girl, with the voice, gestures, and expressions. As she was talking, she went from screaming and reliving the abuse to connecting with me. Then she "switched" into a steely, hard, and viciously determined adversary. She said, "I am going to kill myself, and you can't stop me. Leave me alone!" and headed for the door.

I stopped her, and suddenly she collapsed. Totally unconscious and catatonic. I tried everything to bring her out of it. About to call 911, I stopped since she was safe and began praying silently for God's help.

Suddenly, she quickened but remained in an altered state. She said, "Who is that?" staring off somewhere. Then, "What a nice white Light . . . He's so nice . . ." She began nodding and totally relaxed. After a minute she came to and looked at me, bewildered.

She said, "A white Light came to me and just stood there and surrounded me . . . and I felt safe. And then, he told me, 'Listen to Henry. He will help you. Do what he says. It will be okay.'" She paused, and then said, "It was Jesus."

She was back to her normal state. We continued working until her PTSD was gone. I know some psychologists might say that was just an internal introject, but I have never seen anything like that in many dissociative episodes. It happened the very moment I prayed. He came to her. In many tough moments as she continued recovery, she would recall that moment for hope.

Where in your life right now do you need to remember that when human solutions fail, God's intervention can break through in unexpected ways?

———PRAYER———

Lord God, there are times when I feel completely powerless—when my best efforts fall short and I don't know where to turn. Thank You that You meet us exactly where we are, even in our most broken places. Thank You that Your light can break through any darkness. Help me remember that You're always working, even when everything seems hopeless. When I don't know what to pray, hear my heart's cry for help. In Jesus' name. Amen.

51

Opening Our Eyes to Modern Miracles

Jesus said to them, "My Father is always at his work to this very day, and I too am working. . . . For the Father loves the Son and shows him all he does. Yes, and he will show him even greater works than these, so that you will be amazed." —John 5:17, 20

Have you ever wondered why we don't seem to see the kind of miracles today that we read about in the Bible?

Well, we do.

They literally happen all the time. Friends and missionaries have exposed me to countless things they have experienced and witnessed. Many are readily available in testimonials on YouTube, in web searches, in books, and more. Hundreds of people being fed from one pot of food, like when Jesus fed the five thousand from a few fishes and loaves. People being raised from the dead. Healings of various diseases and maladies. Exorcisms where people are delivered from evil spirits. Vision and hearing restored. Physical creative miracles, such as new eyes being created. Jesus appearing to Muslims and showing them that He is the true God. It is still happening today.

If you are someone who knows God but have not had any or many of those experiences, don't feel like He is any less there or like you are somehow not as spiritual in some sort of way that diminishes your own faith journey or the Presence of God in your life. He works in different ways with all of us.

God also promises something else if you do not know Him yet. He asks you to reach out and seek Him, and He says if you do that, you will find Him.

The question is: When He does show Himself to us, will we see Him? Will we believe and respond?

PRAYER

Father God, thank You that You're still actively working in our world today. I confess that sometimes I doubt or miss seeing Your hand at work. Whether through dramatic miracles or gentle guidance, help me recognize Your Presence in my life. Thank You that You meet each of us differently. Give me eyes to see and a heart ready to respond when You show up in unexpected ways. In Jesus' name. Amen.

52

What If Everything's Not Relative?

Stand firm then, with the belt of truth buckled around your waist, with the breastplate of righteousness in place.

—Ephesians 6:14

You're in a conversation when the other person suggests that what's true for you might not be true for them. Sometimes that's true. Other times it's wrong, and frustrating.

Our close friend was at our house for Sunday brunch with extended family and friends after I had spoken at church. Most were Christians, though she wasn't. We'd been close for years, never letting our different beliefs interfere.

Standing in the kitchen, she said, "You know what I really like about your family's faith? The way it touches your whole life—the family, charities, values, raising kids. It guides so much and does good for you. But what I really like is that you never force it on others."

"Oh my gosh," I said, "I would never want to push it on anyone. Neither does God!"

"Yeah," she said. "Like, it can be true for you, but not true for other people who have their own truth."

"Well, actually, I believe it's not just true for me," I told my friend. "I think it *is* true."

"You mean, like, true-true?" she asked, shocked.

"Yes," I replied. "Not just true for me, but true-true. Like really true."

Looking incredulous, she said, "But . . . there is no such thing as truth."

I paused. "Including that statement?"

She stared at me, then said, "I never thought about it that way."

That moment was profound. Her assertion collapsed upon itself—she stated it like it was true, while claiming nothing is true. I think she realized that some things have to be "true-true."

PRAYER

Father, in a world where everyone has "their truth," thank You that You've given us real truth to stand on. Sometimes I struggle with how to share my faith without pushing it on others. Show me how to love people well while staying anchored to what's real and true. Give me those perfect moments—like that kitchen conversation—where I can help others see Your truth in fresh ways. In Jesus' name. Amen.

53

Is Your Truth THE Truth?

Jesus answered, "I am the way and the truth and the life. No one comes to the Father except through me. If you really know me, you will know my Father as well. From now on, you do know him and have seen him." —John 14:6–7

How comfortable are you with the idea that some truths might be universal rather than personal preferences?

There are ways things are experienced by us, and we carry our perceptions, experiences, and interpretations as our "truth." That is our subjective reality. But there is also external, objective reality.

In my friend's consideration of the "truth" of faith, she treats it as if it is only a "personal truth," having nothing to do with objective truth. But that could be a real problem if there really is a God who exists in objective reality and to whom it matters what we do with Him.

Consider how differently you might approach your conversations about faith if you truly believed you were discussing objective reality rather than exchanging personal opinions.

Along with the friend whose story I've been sharing, I want you to know God. I don't want to try to "convert" in a weird or controlling way, but I want to invite you. That is what God does with us. He doesn't force us; He invites us into a relationship with Him. When I accepted that invitation, my whole world changed. But this is more than just inviting us into a different "truth" for each of us. It is an invitation into what claims to be *the real objective truth about life and the universe.* When people examine Jesus' claims, they find He left zero room for "your truth/my truth" interpretation. According to Him, it cannot be just "true for me." It is true for everyone, or not.

———PRAYER———

Lord, I've grown up in a world that says truth is whatever you want it to be. Yet I know Your truth is not just one option among many, but THE truth that changes everything. Give me wisdom to distinguish between my experiences and Your reality, and the courage to share Your truth with others. In Jesus' name. Amen.

54

Your Faith Can Stand Up to Questions

But examine everything carefully; hold firmly to that which is good. —1 Thessalonians 5:21 NASB

What questions about faith have you been afraid to explore, worried that the answers might undermine your beliefs?

When we consider the claims of Christ, it's not just a preference or another philosophy of life, but His claim to be the ultimate, objective reality with the most significant benefits, and the most serious consequences. He claims not just to be another choice on the buffet, but to be the ultimate objective truth, the one true God.

That day back in college when I walked into the church, I was not looking for the best intellectual argument for some religion or philosophy to live by. I needed God to be "true-true." I needed Him to be objectively real and able to help me.

But after I had begun to follow Him, I had some cognitive dissonance. My head was full of so-called facts like "science disproves the Bible," "there are contradictions in the Bible," "evolution disproves creation," "the church is full of hypocrites," and on and on. Was I finding myself believing in something intellectually indefensible?

Perhaps you've experienced your own moments of cognitive dissonance—that uncomfortable feeling when what you believe seems to conflict with what you know or have been told.

I made a commitment. First, I would seek reconciliation of this as best I could, and second, I would only listen to people who actually knew something and were not just spouting opinions. The short summary of what was a long endeavor is that my questions were satisfied. I found answers to the scientific quandaries, the philosophical questions, the historical questions. I no longer have any cognitive dissonance about believing in Him. I also discovered research showing that a substantial percentage of scientists believe in God, and the number of scientists who believe in a personal God who answers prayer is the same as it was in 1900.

The believing scientists have no cognitive dissonance, either, and most of them are a lot smarter than I am. Ask Francis Collins, the genius who unraveled the DNA code for several diseases, headed up the National Human Genome Research Institute, and converted from atheism to Christianity. He decided as a scientist that he could not reject something without first studying it, so that is what he did. And when he actually studied the evidence, he became a Christian. For him, the evidence came first.

———PRAYER———

Lord, I need You to be real—not just a nice idea or a comforting thought, but actually, objectively real. Sometimes I feel torn between what my heart has experienced and what my mind questions. Give me the courage to dig deeper instead of pushing those questions aside. Help me find genuine answers, just like You helped so many scientists, including Francis Collins. Thank You that You invite both my heart and my mind into relationship with You. In Jesus' name. Amen.

55

When the Facts and Your Faith Dance Together

"For my thoughts are not your thoughts, neither are your ways my ways . . . As the heavens are higher than the earth, so are my ways higher than your ways and my thoughts your thoughts."

—Isaiah 55: 8–9

Which comes more naturally to you—believing with your heart or analyzing with your mind?

I came about this journey in reverse, if you will. Some look at the evidence for Jesus, and then believe that He is real. I jumped in to see if He was there, and then discovered the "evidence" answers. But, either way, both are important to have a vibrant faith; our head and our heart work best when they are on the same team. We need the heart to take the step of faith, and we need the evidence, the Person of Jesus, to have faith "in." He was constantly offering evidence that He was who He said He was, by miracles, by fulfilling prophecies from thousands of years prior concerning the Messiah, by the life He lived, and by His teachings themselves. I found that this was not a "blind" leap of faith I had taken, but an informed one that could stand up to the evidence.

When we study something finite and material, like cell biology, we pursue it to one day "figure it out." But examining the evidence of what exists can never tell us where it came from, or "who" did it.

Even if we're convinced that a Creator must have made our world—and to me there is no other reasonable explanation—once we try to fully understand God, we run into an unavoidable reality: we still will never totally understand Him. While there are many issues He does explain to us, there are many questions about which we ask "Why?" or "How?"

I had struggled with this reality, but then I came to the realization that it could be no other way. If I could totally understand Him, He would not be God.

PRAYER

Father God, thank You for meeting me wherever I am on my faith journey. Whether I come to You through my heart or my head, You're there. I don't need to understand everything about You to trust You completely. Help me rest in that truth today. In Jesus' name. Amen.

56

Finding Balance Between Wonder and Wisdom

When I was a child, I talked like a child, I thought like a child, I reasoned like a child. When I became a man, I put the ways of childhood behind me. For now we see only a reflection as in a mirror; then we shall see face to face. Now I know in part; then I shall know fully, even as I am fully known.

—1 Corinthians 13:11–12

When did you last experience that childlike sense of wonder about God or the world He created?

Research shows that optimists who see the world and the future in a positive light do better and achieve more than pessimists. Even in marriage, couples who see their spouses in a more positive light have better marriages. They retain some of the honeymoon vision: "He is so scattered! Isn't that cute?" versus "What is wrong with you, you idiot?"

Just stay away from extreme denial, don't overlook bad behavior, but keep it positive.

A positive mindset is important, but a childish view of the world is not. At some point, the highest-functioning people are able to deal with what psychologists call dynamic tension. That is the ability to hold polar opposites in tension in your mind and stay away from an "all good" or "all bad" view of self, others, and the world. Mature minds and personalities are able to integrate the good and the bad into one whole that has both.

All-or-nothing thinking, as any psychologist will tell you, not only is immature thinking, but it also keeps us from seeing a lot of reality.

In what areas of your life might you be trapped in all-or-nothing thinking that prevents you from seeing the full reality of God's work in your circumstances?

PRAYER

Father, thank You for the gift of wonder that makes life beautiful. Help me maintain a positive outlook without denying reality. Show me how to appreciate the magic in everyday moments while growing in maturity and understanding. Give me discernment to know when to hold on to childlike faith and when to embrace adult wisdom. In Jesus' name. Amen.

57

How to Find Faith in an Imperfect World

I consider that our present sufferings are not comparable to the glory that will be revealed in us. The creation waits in eager expectation for the revelation of the sons of God. For the creation was subjected to futility, not by its own will, but because of the One who subjected it, in hope that the creation itself will be set free from its bondage to decay and brought into the glorious freedom of the children of God. —Romans 8:18–21 BSB

What aspects of the world's brokenness can make it difficult for you to trust in a good and loving God?

So many obstacles to faith come from our own mindsets versus the mindset of the Bible. I learned this through my dilemmas of faith. I realized I must take the faith as the Bible says it is, and then accept it or reject it accordingly.

What would it mean for your faith journey to embrace both the reality of the world's brokenness *and* the promise of its future redemption?

Earlier, I said God has a marketing problem. If you watch ads on TV or Instagram, they promise you all the good stuff. *Only* the good stuff.

Not this God. He tells us the truth about the world, ourselves, others, and Himself. And lousy marketing as it may seem, it is not all "happy talk." It is the real world as we really see it: both good and bad exist together. No Disneyland fantasy reality. It is *real* reality. In fact, that was one of the things that made me believe even more easily. It hit me that I was looking with my own mindsets of wanting God and the world of the faith to be the way I wanted them to be, versus the way they really are.

We all want the world to be perfect, other people to be perfect, and God to be the God we wish He were. The reason we think that way is because it all *should* be that, and even better than we can imagine. God did create a better life than the one we have. We had it in a perfect Creation, lost it when we left God, but He says it is coming back. And we all, believer or not, long for that lost Eden.

Crap . . . we are in a cognitive dilemma. He made us to think of and long for and groan for a perfect life all the time, a life that does not have pain, poverty, loss, cruelty, bad people, or the like. Just like a hungry person longs for food even when he does not have it, we long for a better world.

PRAYER

God, sometimes I struggle with the gap between what I wish life was and what it actually is. Thank You for being honest with me about reality, even when it's hard to accept. Help me trust that my longings for something better aren't wrong—they're echoes of Eden. Thank You for promising that one day, everything will be made right. Until then, give me courage to embrace faith as it really is. In Jesus' name. Amen.

58

The Faith You're Rejecting Isn't the Faith of the Bible

We know that the whole creation has been groaning together in the pains of childbirth until the present time. Not only that, but we ourselves, who have the firstfruits of the Spirit, groan inwardly as we wait eagerly for our adoption as sons, the redemption of our bodies. For in this hope we were saved; but hope that is seen is no hope at all. Who hopes for what he can already see? But if we hope for what we do not yet see, we wait for it patiently.

—Romans 8:22–29 BSB

Have you ever dismissed Christianity because you couldn't reconcile the idea of a loving God with the suffering you see in the world?

The Bible does not lose that tension. It says the world was created to be ideal, and then when we rejected God, the goodness was infected with evil as a result. Now, from the Bible's explanation, we have both. And that fits reality.

If we are rejecting God because badness exists, we are not rejecting the story of the Bible. We are demanding a world that not only does not exist, but that the Bible does not claim exists, either. It says that both are true.

The good news is that the Bible not only provides a reality picture (that good and bad both exist here), but also tells us that your longing does have an answer, and it will be forthcoming. There is a heaven. There is a Second Coming, where all justice will be served and all things made right that we long to be right.

How might your view of God change if you considered that He grieves the brokenness of this world even more deeply than you do, and is actively working toward its restoration?

PRAYER

God, sometimes I struggle with the tension of believing in Your goodness while seeing so much pain in the world. Help me understand that my longing for perfection comes from You—it's how You designed me. When I get frustrated with the brokenness around me, remind me that this isn't the end of the story. Thank You for promising that one day, You'll make everything right. Until then, help me trust You in the midst of this tension. In Jesus' name. Amen.

59

You Don't Have to Check Your Brain at the Door

The heart of the discerning acquires knowledge, for the ears of the wise seek it out. —Proverbs 18:15

Have you ever felt like choosing faith meant ignoring reason or evidence? I've been there.

After taking the "faith step" in my college awakening, I had nagging questions about what I had done, even as I was experiencing God as real. Many smart people said being a Christian was "intellectual suicide." As someone once said, "If a Christian had a brain cell, it would die of loneliness." My professors were telling us that church teachings were myths. Was I an idiot for believing? I had to reconcile what I was experiencing versus what people were telling me.

As I began investigating, I discovered two things.

First, when I explored the science, I found answers from scientists and other academics. Many scientists, historians, philosophers, and business experts examined the evidence and concluded it supported faith. I learned faith wasn't a matter of "IQ"—many geniuses believe.

Second, much of what was deemed intellectually "indefensible" wasn't what the Bible actually says, but rather misconceptions people had been told or experienced with Christians. What people were rejecting wasn't the real faith—it had more to do with organized religion or common wrongs taught in churches. In fact, I discovered the Bible often agreed with the critics. It was encouraging to find that following Jesus didn't require believing things I knew were goofy.

What intellectual barriers to faith might you be holding on to that are actually based on misconceptions rather than what Christianity actually teaches?

PRAYER

God, sometimes my head and my heart feel like they're in a tug-of-war. Thank You that You don't ask me to shut off my brain to follow You. When I have questions or doubts, help me remember that seeking answers honors You. Give me courage to investigate, wisdom to separate truth from misconceptions, and peace in knowing that authentic faith and honest questions can coexist. Thank You for being bigger than my doubts and patient with my journey. In Jesus' name. Amen.

60

Where Did It All Come From?

By faith we understand that the universe was formed at God's command, so that what is seen was not made out of what was visible. —Hebrews 11:3

When you look at the night sky or consider the vastness of the universe, what does your heart tell you about its origin?

The Bible says there was a beginning to Creation. God spoke all of this into being out of nothing—"ex nihilo." The material universe came from an *immaterial* source, a Person, God. In the Bible's presentation, God, *not this* physical universe, was eternal.

Most atheism says the universe was always there.

The big two options are eternal God or eternal material.

Both believe there was indeed a beginning—the "Big Bang," where and when the universe began. This is important because it shows us how old it is (13.77 billion years is the most believed age) and that it is a finite, expanding universe.

But that logically kills the idea that the universe itself was eternal since astronomers and physicists can show it had a beginning. Everything with a beginning has a cause. The universe had a beginning, so it was not always there.

So, what caused it? It had to be something outside of it, exactly what the Bible says.

After reading all positions, I believe what many astrophysicists and astronomers say: "Someone had to have done this." Those who disagree usually hold fast to their assumption that "since there is no God, it must have happened in a way we don't understand." That's not science, but a faith position, just like believing God did it.

How does your understanding of the beginning of everything shape your perspective on your own purpose and place in this vast universe?

PRAYER

God, when I think about You speaking everything into existence—from galaxies to atoms—I'm filled with awe. Thank You for being the eternal Creator who exists outside of time and space yet cares about my life. Help me see Your fingerprints in both the scientific discoveries and the simple moments of my day. In Jesus' name. Amen.

61

Finding Faith in the Fine-Tuning

They know the truth about God because he has made it obvious to them. For ever since the world was created, people have seen the earth and sky. Through everything God made, they can clearly see his invisible qualities—his eternal power and divine nature. So they have no excuse for not knowing God. Yes, they knew God, but they wouldn't worship him as God or even give him thanks. And they began to think up foolish ideas of what God was like.

—Romans 1:19–21 NLT

Perhaps you've tried to set up a maze of dominoes, realizing how perfectly they have to be arranged to accomplish your goal. How about this: Have you ever marveled at the precision required for our universe to support life?

The next thing I learned about "where did it all come from?" was the reality of the incredible "fine-tuning" of the universe that makes it possible for life to exist. Scientists tell us if you change even a minute detail—a slight alteration to a law of nature or the constants of nature—intelligent life would not have been able to develop.

The next time you look at the night sky or hold a newborn baby, consider the extraordinary precision required for either to exist—does that level of fine-tuning speak to your heart about design or chance?

A. L. Van Den Herik writes about how to explain the fine-tuning of the many physical constants that make up the laws of physics if it just appeared without a Creator. She says, "Astrophysicist Hugh Ross has listed dozens of characteristics of the universe that must be set with extreme precision, such that a minuscule change in any of them would disrupt the balance of the universe enough to prevent it from existing at all. For example, Ross states: 'Unless the number of electrons is equivalent to the number of protons to an accuracy of one part in 1037 or better, electromagnetic forces in the universe would have so overcome gravitational forces that galaxies, stars, and planets never would have formed.'"[*]

I began to think the chances of that happening without a designer in a random explosion takes more faith than I have.

---

* A. L. Van Den Herik, *The Shortest Leap: The Rational Underpinnings of Faith in Jesus*, Kindle Edition (WestBow Press, 2020), citing Hugh Ross, *The Creator and the Cosmos*, 3rd ed. (NavPress, 2001).

When you see design, there has to have been a designer, especially design this complex and precise to subatomic levels.

Even if you had all of the raw material of an unassembled Rolex watch in a paper bag (which is a big assumption even for that to happen by chance . . . having just the right pieces made of just the right metal of just the right shapes, sizes, and weights, all together in a paper bag) and threw them up in the air, the chances of them landing perfectly assembled in working order are not even imaginable. Much less to give you the accurate time that day! And if you find a Rolex watch on the beach, you would not ever think that it formed itself by chance. You naturally would know there was a designer who put all of that together to work the way it works. And that is exactly what the "rocket scientists" themselves say: it had to have a designer.

PRAYER

Father, I'm amazed You balanced every force in the universe just right—from the tiniest atom to the largest galaxy—so that life could exist. Thank You for leaving Your signature on creation in a way that even scientists can recognize. When I doubt, help me remember that the same God who fine-tuned the cosmos also designed me with purpose and loves me personally. Help me respond to Your creative power with worship and gratitude. In Jesus' name. Amen.

62

Why Your Life Isn't Random

In the beginning God created the heavens and the earth. . . . God saw all that he had made, and it was very good.

—Genesis 1:1, 31

Have you ever wondered if your existence is accidental or intentional?

Let's look at a huge problem that exists if you try to explain the earth and life without God—the dependence that all of creation has on systems and interrelatedness, and how those systems could exist without a Designer.

Consider for a moment what it means for your own life if the universe isn't random—if even the most complex systems point to purpose and design rather than chance.

By the way, this has nothing to do with the evolution versus non-evolution debate. (I personally don't care if you think God did it in an instant or if He designed it as a slowly evolving plan. Both positions require Him.)

Let's assume everything started with primordial goo and evolved into greater complexity and complex systems. The question is whether these complex systems could have become like they are without an external designer. Evolutionary scientists of faith say, "God did it" is the only rational explanation, while materialists say, "Evolution must have done it alone since there is no God." Both conclusions require faith.

Design scientists argue that increasing high-order complexity is impossible without a designer. Non-design scientists say it happened through random mutations. One side points to complex systems where parts are dependent on other parts, saying these couldn't have developed without communication. The other shows examples of mutations occurring without design, arguing they could develop into more complex systems through natural selection.

As a layman, the chances of complex systems working together through random mutations, changing DNA to turn a monkey into Einstein with no designer, seems too improbable. Plus, how did organisms exist to write their own reproductive code before they could reproduce? There are many such problems for me with a non-designer viewpoint.

PRAYER

Creator God, sometimes I get caught up in the chaos of life and forget that You designed every detail with purpose—from the stars above to the cells in my body. Thank You for being the master Designer who didn't just wind up the universe and walk away, but who carefully crafted everything to work together. Help me see Your fingerprints in the complexity around me, and remind me that I'm not random—I'm intentionally created by You. In Jesus' name. Amen.

63

Understanding Your Divine Design

How many are your works, LORD! In wisdom you made them all; the earth is full of your creatures. —Psalms 104:24

You may or may not appreciate how the outside of your body looks, but when was the last time you paused to consider the astounding complexity *within* your body?

When I was looking at this design problem in the creation, I would think of systems way simpler than a human, or even a human cell. Take, for example, a car. The engine needs parts designed for one another, just like the human body does. The fuel tank, fuel lines, and fuel pump must work together precisely. Could it be that—just by chance—each part designed itself perfectly to work with other parts?

The carburetor has to mix gas and air perfectly, which is pulled into the cylinder and ignited with perfect timing. The combustion drives the driveshaft, connected to wheels, guided by the steering system. And if you have to stop, there's the braking system, although the brakes didn't know they might be needed one day. Did they evolve themselves randomly, hoping to find a job?

I find this explanation extraordinarily difficult to believe.

Your brain alone has nearly a hundred billion neurons working together. Sensory neurons get information like "you just touched something hot." Motor neurons then command muscles and organs to respond. They communicate through synapses using specific neurotransmitters—not just any chemical mixture will work. Good thing the right chemicals just happened to be there when needed.

To me, all of this developing without a designer is beyond what I have faith to believe.

PRAYER

Father, I'm in awe of Your attention to detail. You carefully designed everything from neurons to galaxies. Thank You for being a God who creates with purpose and precision. When I look at the complexity of Your creation, help me remember that You designed me with the same care and intention. Give me confidence today in knowing I'm part of Your master plan. In Jesus' name. Amen.

64

Your Body's Incredible Design

For you created my inmost being; you knit me together in my mother's womb. I praise you because I am fearfully and wonderfully made; your works are wonderful, I know that full well.

—Psalms 139:13–14

Have you ever thought about what it takes for you to simply see the words you're reading right now?

Eyes let light in. Light comes in through the cornea and hits the lens, and your pupil gets larger or smaller to control the amount of light it lets in (think of a doorman at a bar). The cornea and lens bend the light to make it focus. Light hits the retina, which changes images into electrical signals to the nerves; the optic nerve takes them to the brain's vision area. The optic nerve carries signals from both eyes at once and the brain integrates them into one image. The eye is properly lubricated with window shades and windshield wipers that automatically blink as needed.

Need energy to run this machine of your body? No problem. You have a tongue with taste buds that match the "tastes" available in food. Because you like it, you're motivated to take food in, with anticipation sending messages to produce saliva. You have teeth shaped correctly to process food for swallowing. Your brain sends messengers to your throat to move muscles through the esophagus, skipping your windpipe because the epiglottis manages traffic, into your stomach, which has juices waiting to break the firewood into burnable bits for fuel.

Your system knows what to keep and what to throw away as waste. Your small intestine absorbs water and puts nutrients into your bloodstream that delivers them throughout the body, turning leftover mess into solid stool. That is sent to your rectum until you have a moment to find a magazine and get rid of it.

All of this needed help from other systems, nerves, and hormones. One system of systems of separate parts, working perfectly together, interacting with entire other systems to make just one process required for life work.

What miraculous systems in your body have you been taking for granted, assuming they'll just keep working without acknowledging the extraordinary design behind them?

When I started to look at only an evolutionary process doing all of this without a designer, I just had to cut bait. And, fortunately, I found many scientists who knew way more than me agreeing, on *scientific* grounds, not just common sense. (I am amazed when I hear people say, "I don't believe in God; I believe in 'Science,'" when so many of the scientists they are believing in believe in God!)

PRAYER

Father, I'm blown away when I think about how You engineered every detail of my body. It's amazing how all these systems work together—my brain, my eyes, my stomach, everything—in perfect harmony. Even scientists are in awe of Your design! Help me remember, especially on tough days, that I'm not a cosmic accident. I'm Your masterpiece, carefully crafted by the greatest Designer ever. Thank You for making me so wonderfully complex. In Jesus' name. Amen.

65

From Squeamish About the Bible to Secure

For we did not follow cleverly devised stories when we told you about the coming of our Lord Jesus Christ in power, but we were eyewitnesses of his majesty. —2 PETER 1:16

You've probably been there. I have. Surrounded by skeptical voices, you start to feel a bit uncomfortable or embarrassed about your faith.

Back in college, I frequently carried a Bible with my stack of books. I knew everyone was looking at me like I was a superstitious idiot. I had to admit to feeling a bit squeamish.

I could walk in there today and not feel squeamish at all for one simple reason: I feel very secure about the Bible being true. But that change didn't happen overnight. It was a process of lots of study and learning how dependable the Bible actually is and, over time, how much it continues to be proven trustworthy.

I want to share with you just a little of what I learned in my early days of faith that taught me to trust it as God's Word to us.

My beginning question, and it was a big one, was whether I could trust the Scripture as truth. For instance, how do we know the New Testament record is true?

One way is by knowing when it was written.

Critics used to say that so much time had passed between when Jesus actually lived and when the New Testament was written that the story morphed and contains a lot of myths in it. Actually, archaeology has proven that wrong. Some of the world's foremost archaeologists affirm that the documents of the New Testament could not be from the second century, but instead that every book of the New Testament was written between the forties and eighties of the first century, probably before the fall of Jerusalem in AD 70.

This is a big deal because it means the records of the life of Jesus and the facts surrounding His miracles, resurrection, and teachings were written and widely distributed while eyewitnesses were still alive. Imagine major newspapers and television networks reporting that Taylor Swift had claimed to be God and the Messiah and performed many miracles and rose from the dead after being crucified by the record industry in Times Square *while people who lived in New York City are still around.* All of those people in New

York who knew that to not be true would kill the story, and for sure, you would read many, many other articles talking about how false it was.

PRAYER

Father, thank You for preserving Your Word through history and giving us so many reasons to trust it. When I feel uncertain or face skepticism from others, remind me that Your Word isn't just ancient stories—it's Your living truth, backed by real evidence and eyewitness accounts. Help me grow more confident in Your Word each day and give me wisdom to share this confidence with others who might be struggling with similar doubts. In Jesus' name. Amen.

66

Why You Can Trust What You're Reading

Many have undertaken to draw up an account of the things that have been fulfilled among us, just as they were handed down to us by those who from the first were eyewitnesses and servants of the word. With this in mind, since I myself have carefully investigated everything from the beginning, I too decided to write an orderly account for you, most excellent Theophilus, so that you may know the certainty of the things you have been taught.

—Luke 1:1–4

Have you ever been asked how you can know that what we read in the Bible today accurately reflects what was written thousands of years ago? Yeah, me too.

There were many other reasons I became confident that the Bible is true and trustworthy.

One is that Jesus' followers were beginning a movement and were being persecuted and dying because they said it is true. Think about it: dying for it when you knew you *hadn't* seen it happen? Many of the early eyewitnesses to Jesus being alive after His resurrection went on to be tortured and killed for holding on to their account of what they had seen.

And we can be confident that's really what happened, because the Bible writings describing it come to us from twenty to fifty years after it happened, way too short of a period of time to allow corruption of the original content. As of this writing, that would be like making up stories about Michael Jordan that are mythical fabrications and selling them as things that really happened. People were there and know better.

The gospels clearly pass the tests that we use to scrutinize any writings of antiquity. No one doubts Aristotle's writings, and the earliest copy we have of those were nearly 1,400 years after his death, and only forty-nine manuscripts exist. We only have nine or ten copies of Caesar's history of the Gallic Wars, dating a thousand years after his death. At this time, there are *over 5,600* Greek manuscripts of the New Testament that have been found.

I believe the Bible is a trustworthy record of the life of Jesus and the story of God. If we can trust anything from the literature of antiquity, we can trust the Bible. In addition, there are many extra-biblical (non-biblical) secular historians writing at the same time who talk about Jesus and the movement (see for example, Josephus, Tacitus, Pliny the Younger, Phlegon, Thallus, Suetonius, Lucian, et cetera). Even if you don't want to believe in the Bible, you still have to deal with Jesus, because the historians of His time were writing about Him as well.

PRAYER

Father, thank You not asking me to take a blind leap of faith. You've given us solid reasons to trust the Bible's reliability—from the early Christians who died defending what they saw, to thousands of ancient manuscripts that confirm these accounts. When doubts creep in, remind me that Your Word has stood up to centuries of scrutiny. Help me share this confidence with others who are searching for truth. In Jesus' name. Amen.

67

How Can You Be Sure Jesus Is Really the One?

Beginning with Moses and all the Prophets, he explained to them what was said in all the Scriptures concerning himself.

—Luke 24:27

Here's something you may never have considered: What is the mathematical probability of one person fulfilling hundreds of specific prophecies written centuries before their birth?

The entire Bible points to one Person: Jesus the Messiah. The Jews of the first century were among many waiting for the foretold Messiah. When Jesus appeared claiming "I am He," how were they—and we—to know He was the one?

Jesus fulfilled all the Old Testament Messianic prophecies. He fulfilled around three hundred specific prophecies written long before His arrival. Some examples:

- Born of a virgin
- Born in Bethlehem

- Preceded by a messenger (John the Baptist)
- Triumphantly enter Jerusalem on a donkey
- Betrayed by His friend for thirty silver pieces (Judas)
- Crucified with specific wounds
- Clothes divided by casting lots
- Buried with the rich (the tomb given by Joseph of Arimathea)

And many, many, many more.

As you read through those prophecies Jesus fulfilled, which ones stand out to you as the most compelling evidence that He was exactly who He claimed to be?

It became clear to me that only a supernatural book inspired by God could make that many predictions that were fulfilled by one specific person. It was just one more building block that said to me this book was the real deal.

PRAYER

Father, I'm amazed at how You wove Your story together across centuries, leaving clues that all led to Jesus. Help me trust that the same God who fulfilled hundreds of prophecies is still working in my life today. In Jesus' name. Amen.

68

Making Sense of the Bible's "Contradictions"

Now the Berean Jews were of more noble character than those in Thessalonica, for they received the message with great eagerness and examined the Scriptures every day to see if what Paul said was true. —Acts 17:11

Have apparent contradictions in the Bible ever made you doubt its reliability or accuracy?

That's why I decided that next, I had to research the apparent contradictions in the Bible. When I did, it became clear to me that they are readily understandable, such as different eyewitness accounts that tell a different view of the same incident. Think about how you might tell a story differently than your friend who experienced the same event—would those differences make either of you untrustworthy, or simply show you noticed or emphasized different details?

Nowhere in the Bible is there a contradiction of the central message or important points. One gospel writer might report a different number of angels than the other at the tomb. If I saw you and a few other people at a concert, I might say to a mutual friend, “I saw Heather at the concert.” A friend who was with me might tell someone, “I saw Heather and Sarah at the concert.” No contradiction other than what one emphasizes versus another. But never in the Bible do you see someone saying, “He died and was placed in a tomb” and someone else saying, “He didn’t die after the cross, he went fishing.” Those kinds of contradictions are not there, the kind that would make us question the main message it is trying to convey.

Others argue that we can’t trust the Bible because there are “so many translations.” But they are all translated from the original language, and the originals are what they are, period.

A similar criticism some people have is about different denominations and theologians believing very different things. There are different denominations . . . that is true . . . in some ways. For all of the “denominations” who fall into what is called “orthodox,” believe in the same essentials of the faith and agree on them. All those denominations agree on 90 percent of the rest of the “main” message.

The Bible itself says people will disagree on some minor issues, what is called “disputable” issues (Rom. 14:1), and allows for it, as long as they believe the essentials: Jesus is who

He said He was, died, and was resurrected, and we are reconnected to God through believing in Him. That is the gospel.

PRAYER

Father, I'm grateful for Your Word and how it all points to Jesus. When I struggle with questions or doubts, remind me that You're not afraid of my honest searching. Thank You that the core message of the gospel stands firm across every translation and denomination. Help me to study Your Word carefully but always remember that the goal isn't just knowledge—it's knowing You better. In Jesus' name. Amen.

69

Are Biblical Miracles Just Ancient History?

"Believe me when I say that I am in the Father and the Father is in me; or at least believe on the evidence of the works themselves. Very truly I tell you, whoever believes in me will do the works I have been doing, and they will do even greater things than these, because I am going to the Father. And I will do whatever you ask in my name, so that the Father may be glorified in the Son. You may ask me for anything in my name, and I will do it."

—John 14:11–14

Do you believe God still performs miracles today, or do you think they were limited to biblical times?

As a kid, I was told the miracles in the Bible were true, but God didn't do that stuff anymore. Those were for "biblical times." Now we have doctors so we don't need God for healing. And the miracles were for Jesus to prove who He said He was. That was fine with me, since I just wanted to play golf.

But when I got serious about this stuff and based my life on it all being true, I had to ask, "What about all of these miracles? And why wouldn't He continue to do miracles today? What gives?"

I found out.

Why don't we see the things we read about in the Bible occurring today? The answer is, "We do." They happen every day around the world. They literally happen all the time and are easily findable. My first source back then was reading books containing spiritual memoirs and personal journeys that gave accounts of all sorts of miracles, just like in the Bible. Then I began to go to churches to hear speakers tell their stories and testimonies. I also began to hear about an abundance of miracles when I started to work with mission's organizations.

Incredible miracles do happen today, all over the world. You will find some who have other interpretations of those events, like my friend to whom I told the kneecap healing story, and he said it was just the power of my mind that did that. Really? My mind conjured up something about a kneecap and the next day sent electricity to someone I had never seen who just happened to be in the audience and his infection was healed? His interpretation takes faith, it seems to me.

But as for me, I am like the blind man whom He healed and came back unable to explain it, but said, "But I know this: I was blind, and now I can see" (John 9:25 NLT)! I can't explain it all, either, but I have known miracles in my life.

What would it take for you to recognize a miracle in your own life—and are you open to the possibility that what you've dismissed as coincidence might actually be divine intervention?

PRAYER

Jesus, sometimes I struggle to believe You're still in the miracle business. Maybe I've gotten too comfortable with my rational explanations, or maybe I'm afraid to expect too much. But Your Word promises You're still working, still healing, still showing up in powerful ways. There are ample testimonies of Your miracles all around the world, evey day. Help me to approach You with childlike faith, ready to see Your power at work in my life and in our world today. In Jesus' name. Amen.

70

The Most Important Fact in the Bible

And if Christ has not been raised, our preaching is useless and so is your faith. More than that, we are then found to be false witnesses about God, for we have testified about God that he raised Christ from the dead. But he did not raise him if in fact the dead are not raised. For if the dead are not raised, then Christ has not been raised either. And if Christ has not been raised, your faith is futile; you are still in your sins. —1 Corinthians 15:14–17

The singular most important fact in the Bible is also the biggest hurdle for many people: the resurrection of Jesus.

Have you ever considered that your stance on this single historical question—did Jesus rise from the dead?—ultimately determines your response to everything else about Christianity and maybe even life?

It should be the big question. The apostle Paul said if the resurrection were not true, not only were he and the rest of them liars, but the whole faith is worth nothing.

The entire New Testament's message about who Jesus is rests upon one question: Did He "true-true" rise from the dead? If He did, then it proves that He was the Messiah, and if He didn't, then we are to be the most pitied of all people . . . following a faith based on a fairy tale. But Paul, having experienced Jesus in his radical conversion on the Damascus Road, had no doubt, so much so that he spent the rest of his life traveling throughout that world proclaiming the gospel of Jesus, even when being beaten, persecuted, imprisoned, and finally killed.

Throughout the New Testament, the resurrection is the front and center issue, as it not only showed that Jesus was the Messiah, but also validated that He had accomplished His mission of overcoming death itself, both spiritual and physical.

So, the evidence for the resurrection is paramount.

You can't have a resurrection without a death. His crucifixion and death were attested to not only by the Bible but also by secular historians and writers—Josephus, Tacitus, Lucian, and the Jewish Talmud all write about His crucifixion. The Bible consistently refers to it and to the testimonies of those who were there and knew about it.

There is no account in history of anyone ever surviving a Roman crucifixion. No one disputes that He was crucified, but some try to say that He was really not dead. But there is no account anywhere to say that He was not, and no one has ever survived a crucifixion. He was, in fact, dead.

PRAYER

Lord, I'll be honest—sometimes the resurrection seems almost too amazing to believe. But I'm grateful for the evidence You've left us, both in Your Word and in history. Thank You that my faith isn't based on wishful thinking but on historical fact. Like Paul, help me to live as though this changes everything—because it does. Let the reality of Your resurrection power fill me with hope and purpose today. In Jesus' name. Amen.

71

He Is Alive, and That Changes Everything

For what I received I passed on to you as of first importance: that Christ died for our sins according to the Scriptures, that he was buried, that he was raised on the third day according to the Scriptures, and that he appeared to Cephas, and then to the Twelve. After that, he appeared to more than five hundred of the brothers and sisters at the same time, most of whom are still living, though some have fallen asleep. Then he appeared to James, then to all the apostles, and last of all he appeared to me also, as to one abnormally born. —1 Corinthians 15:3–8

How different would your life be if Jesus hadn't risen from the dead?

The accounts of what happened on that first Easter morning are sound. The tomb had been sealed and guarded, and yet . . . He was gone.

Even the opponents of the empty tomb agreed that it was empty . . . they said, "The disciples stole the body."

Then Jesus started appearing.

There were many eyewitnesses. Not only His disciples, but other followers and also the authors of New Testament books, as well as sources outside the New Testament, all attest to the resurrection. Witnesses attest to His appearing to over five hundred people. These witnesses turned into bold evangelists, ready to do anything to tell others about this risen Christ. The movement began to spread because of them.

They continued in this message, even though they were persecuted and many were killed because of their testimony. Those deaths are written about by extra-biblical writers as well. It is hard to believe that so many people would die for what they knew was a lie. I am sure someone would have finally given in and said, “Okay, just kidding, if you are going to kill me.” But they kept on, right to their deaths. But they did not die for a lie . . . they died because they knew that He had risen from the dead.

In examining the historical evidence for what the Bible says about the resurrection, I came to the conclusion that what I was experiencing was not only true for me, but it was “true-true” history. This cognitive dissonance for me was settled. And in the years since, I can continue to attest through my own experience, He is alive. He was, in fact, raised.

PRAYER

Jesus, thank You for not leaving us with just blind faith, but giving us solid evidence through hundreds of witnesses who saw You alive. When doubts creep in, remind me of those early believers who staked their lives on Your resurrection. Help me live with the same certainty they had—not because someone told me to believe, but because the evidence is clear: You are alive, and that changes everything. Help me to connect with You today, since You are alive and with me. In Jesus' name. Amen.

72

The Christians Who Create the Bad Christian Stereotypes

Live such good lives among the pagans that, though they accuse you of doing wrong, they may see your good deeds and glorify God on the day he visits us. —1 Peter 2:12

Do you have a friend or family member who has negative views of Christians based on hurtful experiences?

That was another obstacle I had to get around—that some Christians live in a way that can lead us to doubt Jesus.

A number of years ago, we had a new family move in next door to us. It was an instant connection—we both had new baby girls, the husband and I had both just begun new businesses, so we were in the same phases of life.

After a few weeks, we invited them over for dinner. When I asked the wife about her family, she began telling us about where she grew up and her parents and siblings. Then her demeanor totally changed. She said, "And then . . . also . . . I have one sister who is one of those crazy Christians.

You know . . . the 'born-again' type. That stuff drives me nuts!"

I nodded, and just said, "Yeah . . . I know what you mean."

"So, you know some of them too?" she asked.

"Oh, yeah. I know lots of them," I replied, and she returned to more accounts of her experiences with "crazy Christians."

I couldn't help but agree with much of what she said about her experiences with Christians. They ranged from stupid to outright hurtful. I felt embarrassed. But what stood out most was the crappy bind I felt. I would love to talk about my faith with her—or anyone else. I want to share the love and reality of God with others. But I couldn't do that, because she had already developed a view of what a Christian was. I knew anything I said wouldn't put much of a dent in that view. I would just suddenly be one of those "nutcases."

The sad reality is that many of those views are learned for very good reason. People have sometimes been hurt by a Christian or a church, maybe severely. They have known hypocrites, been lied to or swindled, or just seen a "Christian" who was worse than unlikable and maybe even mean.

Perhaps you've been on either side of this experience—feeling misrepresented by other believers, or forming judgments about faith based on someone's poor example.

PRAYER

Father, my heart breaks for people who've been hurt by those claiming to follow You. I know I'm not perfect either, but I want to help heal those wounds, not deepen them. Give me patience when I encounter skepticism and help me respond with genuine love and understanding. Show me how to be authentic about my faith without pushing people away. Help me demonstrate what following Jesus really looks like. In Jesus' name. Amen.

73

Finding God Beyond the People Who Misrepresent Him

"Do not become a stumbling block, whether to Jews or Greeks or the church of God—as I also try to please everyone in all I do. For I am not seeking my own good, but the good of many, that they may be saved." —1 Corinthians 10:32–33 BSB

Have painful experiences with religious people ever created barriers between you and God?

Think of having a parent who talks about God but then treats you like crap. Or worse, a pastor or youth worker or priest who molests you. Or a husband who claims the name of Jesus and is abusive. Sadly, what we know of God is influenced by who we know of God.

I would love for my friends to know my faith experience, not just their experience of people who have hurt or not been good to them.

I was under contract to speak at a secular worldwide leadership event, broadcasted to arenas. Many of the biggest companies in the world would be attending, and I had spoken there several times before. The arena in this particular city was controlled by city permits, and because someone on the city council associated me with someone else's "Christian" views, they not only banned *me*, but would not allow the *event* to take place in their arena because I was "one of those." I never found out specifically what happened, but apparently, someone on that city's leadership council had had some negative experiences with Christians that tainted their view of what I was going to be like. Guilt by association.

God doesn't want anyone getting in the way of your being able to see Him for who He is, and if that has ever happened to you, I am sorry. Give Him another chance.

PRAYER

Father, I'm struggling with the gap between what people say about You and how they act. When I see Christians hurting others or misrepresenting You, it makes me angry and confused. Help me find the real You in the midst of all this mess. Give me discernment to recognize authentic faith when I see it, and the courage to keep seeking You even when Your followers disappoint me. Thank You that You're bigger than human failures. In Jesus' name. Amen.

74

Jesus Versus Judgment

"Do not judge, and you will not be judged. Do not condemn, and you will not be condemned. Forgive, and you will be forgiven."

—Luke 6:37

When you hear the word "Christian," does it bring to mind grace and forgiveness, or judgment and guilt? How do you think most people would answer that question?

I was talking to a contractor and he was telling me about growing up around a particular church where the youth group had a big presence in his neighborhood. He said that after being around them, he didn't want anything to do with church or God, as they were always telling him how "bad" he was. We all probably can relate to that feeling of being looked down upon by self-righteous religious people.

We moved to a new neighborhood when our daughters were just born, and one Sunday morning I was loading them into the car when my neighbor said, "Morning . . . where are y'all headed?"

"Church," I replied. "Want to come?"

"Are you kidding?" she said. "No way."

"How come?"

"I can't take the guilt!"

I remember thinking, *How did a faith whose founder, Jesus, literally came to end guilt forever with a message of forgiveness become the Walmart of selling guilt?*

Listen to what Jesus said: "For I did not come to judge the world, but to save the world" (John 12:47).

Over and over, He stood against those religious people who judged others. Once, when a woman was caught in adultery and the church leaders brought her to Jesus to be judged, saying she should be stoned, He said, "Let any one of you who is without sin be the first to throw a stone at her" (John 8:7).

How might others' perception of faith change if you emphasized the same grace-filled priorities Jesus did?

PRAYER

God, sometimes I feel worn down by all the religious "should"s and expectations. Help me grasp the difference between genuine faith and empty religiosity. When I'm tempted to judge others or beat myself up, remind me of Your grace. Thank You that You meet my imperfection with love, not condemnation. In Jesus' name. Amen.

75

What Does Real Faith Look Like?

"By their fruit you will recognize them. Not everyone who says to me, 'Lord, Lord,' will enter the kingdom of heaven, but only the one who does the will of my Father who is in heaven."

—Matthew 7:20–21

What behaviors do you think would stand out in someone who genuinely lives their faith?

There really are many very good Christians out there—truly loving, giving, honest and responsible ones. These are the "mature" ones the Bible speaks of who bear "good fruit."

Here's how the Bible describes true faith: "Pure and undefiled religion before our God and Father is this: to care for orphans and widows in their distress, and to keep oneself from being polluted by the world" (James 1:27 BSB).

God describes what genuine faith looks like: "Isn't it to share your bread with the hungry, to bring the poor and homeless into your home, to clothe the naked when you see him, and not to turn away from your own flesh and blood" (Isa. 58:7 BSB)?

The Bible contrasts two paths: "The acts of the flesh are obvious: sexual immorality, impurity and debauchery; idolatry and witchcraft; hatred, discord, jealousy, fits of rage, selfish ambition, dissensions, factions and envy; drunkenness, orgies, and the like. I warn you, as I did before, that those who live like this will not inherit the kingdom of God. But the fruit of the Spirit is love, joy, peace, forbearance, kindness, goodness, faithfulness, gentleness and self-control. Against such things there is no law" (Gal. 5:19–23).

Compare the people you know who are like the first list versus the ones who are like the second. True faith is not hard to spot. I had a friend who was listing all of her objections to the faith, because of the bad behavior of some. I said, "Good news! The Bible agrees with you! And not only that, you agree with it, too, about what the good things in life are!"

"Like what?" she asked.

"Well, like the stuff you care about: love, responsibility, freedom, honesty, justice, compassion, forgiveness, second chances, developing and using your talents, having purpose, relationships, giving, parties and celebrations, family, deep friendships . . . That's pretty much what the whole book is about. That is what the Bible says God wants us to be like."

PRAYER

Lord, sometimes I get discouraged when I see people claiming to follow You but acting badly. Help me focus instead on the beautiful examples of true faith around me. Guide me to be one of those people who shows Your love through concrete actions—caring for others, showing compassion, and living with integrity. Shape my heart to bear the fruit of Your Spirit. Thank You for showing me what real faith looks like. In Jesus' name. Amen.

76

Wrestling with God

My God, my God, why have you forsaken me? Why are you so far from saving me, so far from my cries of anguish? —Psalm 22:1

You may feel like questioning God's goodness or power makes you a bad Christian. It doesn't. It makes you human.

In one sense, God was easy for me to believe in. All I had to do was look at the sky at night or read a neurology book. At the same time, some facts made it hard to believe, like "Why were some Christians and churches so mean?"

Where in your own life have you struggled to reconcile your belief in a loving God with painful experiences that seem to contradict that belief?

But there is one obstacle that rises above all the rest as the most difficult: If God is loving and good and all-powerful and could end all suffering, why do we have it? How can a loving God allow this to go on? Where is He? For me, that is the really hard one.

I had very close friends who lost their son to a rare childhood cancer. I was very close to him and they are like family to me. He was young, talented, gifted, loving, a person of faith, and had an incredible future in front of him. I could not stand it that he got sick and died.

Part of what made it too much was the injustice of it all—not only for him but his parents. I have never known better people, whose entire life was spent helping others. While no one deserves this, they especially did not deserve this. Here they are, living a lifetime of sacrifice and service, and this is what they get. I just could not make it work.

The assumption most of us make is that if God were really good and compassionate, and truly all-powerful, He would get rid of all the pain and suffering in the world.

Ironically, the answer I was looking for was found in the love of God. The very thing that I was doubting is where I found the answer. Suffering does not mean that God loves us less. It actually points to how huge He loves us. God's love for us is so great that He gives us freedom. And when you study the problem of evil, suffering, and a good God, I have come to understand what love requires to exist: freedom. Tomorrow we'll dig in to why freedom is so necessary.

PRAYER

Father, there are days when I struggle to reconcile Your goodness with the pain I see around me. Thank You that You're big enough to handle my doubts and questions. When suffering feels overwhelming, help me remember that You gave us freedom because You love us that much. Give me peace when I don't have answers, and hope when I can't see the bigger picture. In Jesus' name. Amen.

77

Why Real Love Requires Freedom

Now the Lord is the Spirit, and where the Spirit of the Lord is, there is freedom. —2 Corinthians 3:17

What if the freedom to reject God might actually be one of His greatest gifts of love?

God loves us and wants us to love Him back. The entire Bible can be seen as a love story between God and His created beings—a romance broken by our rejection of God.

God designed us to love Him, but love requires freedom of choice. If we are not free and lack true free will, we cannot have love. When controlled in a relationship and forced to love someone because we have no choice, that is not love but slavery. Freedom is essential for love to exist.

God did not want to receive "love" from robots who had to love and obey Him. He wanted the real thing.

So, God gave us complete freedom to love and obey Him or turn from Him. He trusted us to run the earth, to love Him and each other, to nurture Creation. It was a serious act of love—giving us all this and setting us free to either care for it and love Him back or reject Him.

However, freedom means real consequences. He warned: "If you eat of the tree of the knowledge of good and evil, you will die." We were never supposed to know both good and evil. To be separated from Life (God) is death.

We chose to separate from God, and now we experience "death" daily—in relationships, the world around us, governments, families, our bodies, and every aspect of creation. Our existence, as good as it can be sometimes, is marred by this disease called death, which is separation from God.

So, God loved us so much to give us freedom, and we chose against Him. We ran away from home. And it did not work out well at all. Today, that is the world that we live in.

PRAYER

God, it amazes me that You trust me with free will. You could force my love, but You don't. Instead, You invite me into a genuine relationship. I confess that sometimes I've used this freedom to choose my own way instead of Yours. Thank You for continuing to love me anyway. Help me use my freedom today to choose You, to love You, and to love others the way You intended. In Jesus' name. Amen.

78

How About the Hypocrites?

Anyone who does not do what is right is not God's child, nor is anyone who does not love their brother and sister. . . . Anyone who does not love remains in death. —1 John 3:10, 14

Has someone's hypocrisy ever created a roadblock to your own faith journey?

Christians who do terrible things while claiming faith raise valid questions. If faith should make us more loving and better people, how can it be true when some Christians behave so badly? How might your approach to church and faith communities change if you expected to find both genuine believers and counterfeits mixed together?

God actually tells us His church will be a mixed group—after all, the membership requirement is being a sinner. He warns that impostors will enter too.

Jesus addressed this directly in the parable of the weeds: "No . . . if you pull the weeds now, you might uproot the wheat with them. Let both grow together until the harvest. At that time I will tell the harvesters: First collect the weeds and tie them in bundles to be burned; then gather the wheat into my barn" (Matt. 13:29–30 BSB).

He further warned: "Not everyone who says to Me, 'Lord, Lord,' will enter the kingdom of heaven, but only he who does the will of My Father in heaven. Many will say to Me on that day, 'Lord, Lord, did we not prophesy in Your name, and in Your name drive out demons and perform many miracles?' Then I will tell them plainly, 'I never knew you; depart from Me'" (Matt. 7:21–23 BSB).

The Bible acknowledges false teachers seeking power and money will make faith look bad, but those who consistently act unlovingly prove they're not truly God's children.

Bottom line: Do not be surprised by bad, unloving people in the church, but *expect* it. He *told* us they would be there. He also said to learn to recognize them.

PRAYER

Dear God, I admit I sometimes get angry and discouraged when I see "Christians" behaving badly. Thank You for being honest with us about this reality in Your Word. Please help me respond with Your wisdom—not becoming cynical, but also not being naive. Show me how to stay focused on loving You and others genuinely, while being discerning about false teaching and hypocrisy. Make me part of the solution. Keep me from being a person who claims You, but doesn't do Your will by loving others. In Jesus' name. Amen.

79

Real Love Requires Risk

See what great love the Father has lavished on us, that we should be called children of God! And that is what we are! —1 John 3:1

Have you ever looked back at your life and realized some of your best growth has come through having the freedom to make your own choices—even mistakes?

As a psychologist, I am very troubled when I see "helicopter" parenting. It hurts children's development. They need to be free to grow, to choose, even if that freedom is risky, and they fall down and hurt themselves, because they then learn to not fall down!

If you are a parent, you do what God did. You give your children freedom to be themselves, and you do not stand there turning them into little overcontrolled robots. You give them the rules: "Stay in the yard, don't hit each other, stay out of the thorny bushes." Or, if they are older, "Don't believe the tempter who says the drugs are good and won't hurt you." If they obey you, they will be fine.

God was not willing to make robots. He loves us. He is a loving parent. He wanted humans to love. And to be human, to be in His image, you have to be free. Free to follow Him and stay connected to all that is good and alive, or separate from Him and Life and experience the pain of "knowing good and evil."

Some will ask, "If God knew that would happen and that people would end up suffering, then why did He go ahead and create the risk?" He wanted a relationship with humans so much, to share love with us being free to love Him back, that He was willing to do it. Even if it meant things would go bad and there would be suffering and loss. To have love, He had to make us free to "not love."

PRAYER

God, it amazes me that You chose to risk everything just to have a real relationship with me. I see now how much trust that took—like a parent watching their child take those first wobbly steps. Thank You for giving me space to grow, for setting loving boundaries, and for being there when I fall. Help me to use my freedom wisely and to choose love—both for You and others. Thank You for being such a good Father. In Jesus' name. Amen.

80

Jesus, the Real Plan All Along

"And hope does not put us to shame, because God's love has been poured out into our hearts through the Holy Spirit, who has been given to us. You see, at just the right time, when we were still powerless, Christ died for the ungodly. Very rarely will anyone die for a righteous person, though for a good person someone might possibly dare to die. But God demonstrates his own love for us in this: While we were still sinners, Christ died for us."

—Romans 5:5–8

Have you ever wondered if God was caught off guard by humanity's failures, or if He had a plan all along?

As much as He wanted freedom for us, and as much as He knew we would misuse it, He had an option available to Him that we don't have. Knowing what He knew, He had an even bigger plan, where the pain and suffering would not win in the end after all. What does it mean for your own struggles and failures to know that God anticipated them from the beginning and has already set in motion a plan for redemption?

He loves us so much that He wasn't going to leave us and this world in the mess of our rejection of Him. Like any good, loving parent, He never gives up on His children, never abandons us, and searches for us to bring us back into connection and fix what we have broken.

He had a plan B that would end up with good winning over all of the evil in the end. His plan B had a name: Jesus. And it was the real plan A all along, because He knew we would use our freedom poorly. He says in Genesis 3 that there would be a Savior, born of the seed of woman, who would be compelled by love to come rescue us, to crush the works of the tempter, and bring back all of those who want to come back to life.

In the crucifixion, Jesus reversed what we had broken. He was struck on the heel . . . "wounded," but not a final death blow. He was resurrected to life. But the tempter's work was crushed on the head. It was fatal. Death died the day of the resurrection of Jesus.

God wins. He gets what He wanted all along: a love relationship with His humans who really want Him. Even when it all went bad, He had a plan that would bring it all back to good, for all who want to come.

So, while we do live in a world with pain and suffering, for me, there is a good explanation as to why. God gave us freedom, and we chose against life. The result is a world that is experiencing death. But thankfully, getting reconnected saved my life.

But even with that, and even with my accepting the reality of free will, another truth was and still is hard for me to accept as well: Why so long? Why does He let it go on?

More on that tomorrow.

PRAYER

God, it amazes me that You knew exactly what would happen, yet You chose to create me anyway. You loved me enough to let me choose and loved me enough to rescue me when my choices went wrong. Thank You for Jesus—not just Your backup plan, but Your perfect plan all along. When I struggle with the "why" questions, help me remember Your heart of love. Give me patience to trust Your timing. In Jesus' name. Amen.

81

Trusting God's Heart When Life Hurts

"Though he slay me, yet I will hope in him." —Job 13:15

What questions about suffering keep you up at night, searching for answers that seem just out of reach?

God had a plan to make it all perfect again, and one day that will be complete. We get glimpses of His healing now, but He is not doing it all fully right now. We still suffer, and there is unspeakable evil in the world. Even after Jesus came and was resurrected. Why does He allow it to continue? Why is there suffering in this age between the fall of the earth and its final redemption? Why doesn't He just fix it all now?

The answer I found? There is not one. At least not one that fully satisfies.

Where in your journey have you had to choose between demanding answers and simply trusting God's character when life made no sense?

If God is infinitely loving, good, powerful, and just, then there must be an answer. He would do nothing evil or unjust or unloving. He is Love, fairness, and compassion. I am certain He knows why He has allowed this season of suffering until Jesus comes back and makes it all new again. But why the "wait till then" approach? I am sure He knows why He is doing it this way—it just doesn't make sense to me.

The Bible says there is no answer He will give us other than "Trust Me." That is the only real answer besides His promise to make it all right in the end.

Job's story illustrates this best. He was "blameless," yet God allowed him to suffer horribly. He lost his health, possessions, respect, and worst of all, his children. His suffering was so extreme that he wished he had never been born. His friends wrongly blamed him for his suffering, but Job never turned away from God. Though he raged and argued, he still trusted God's goodness, saying "Though he slay me, yet I will hope in him" (Job 13:15).

When God finally answered Job, He simply said His wisdom and understanding were far beyond Job's comprehension. He listed His mighty works of creation and asked, "Who are you to question Me?" He didn't give the answer Job wanted, but showed He was Someone who knew the answer.

Job's final response was: "I had only heard about you before, but now I have seen you with my own eyes. I take back everything I said" (Job 42:5–6 NLT).

God never answers the "why" question. He gives us a "Who" answer. It comes down to faith in God—trusting Who He is, even when we don't understand why. And for Job, that was enough.

PRAYER

Father, in my moments of doubt and pain, draw me closer to Your heart. When I struggle to make sense of suffering—my own or others'—remind me that You are the God who sees, knows, and cares. Though I may not understand Your timing or Your ways, help me trust in Your perfect wisdom and unfailing love. Like Job, let me come to know You more deeply through my struggles, until seeing You becomes enough. In Jesus' name. Amen.

82

When You Have Unanswered Questions

At noon, darkness came over the whole land until three in the afternoon. And at three in the afternoon Jesus cried out in a loud voice, "Eloi, Eloi, lema sabachthani?" (which means "My God, my God, why have you forsaken me?"). —Mark 15:33–34

Have you ever felt abandoned by God in the middle of your pain?

When Jesus was on the cross, He said, "My God, My God, why have You forsaken Me?"

Jesus, in His humanity, felt the same way we do. He could not understand why His Father seemingly had forsaken Him. But God *did* understand why, and behind it all, God was still all loving, all-powerful, and all good.

I did not emotionally accept this truth until my training as a psychologist, when I learned about how our cognitive understanding works. A child literally cannot understand certain things until she gets to a higher level of ability to understand. Her mind just cannot wrap itself around something too high for it to make sense.

A very young child is taken to the doctor and gets a painful shot. She screams at her parent: "How can you let this happen to me? If you love me, how can you let this happen?" All the while, the parent does understand the "why" and knows that he or she loves that child as much as is possible. They know the suffering is not because they do not love their little one. They get it, even when the child does not.

When I can't understand why He sometimes allows horrible things to happen, I can accept that I do not understand, nor do I have an answer for that. I can accept that I have limited understanding. But I do believe He has reasons for waiting to end all suffering that I am just not big enough to comprehend. His ways are above my ways, as the Bible says, and His thoughts are above my thoughts. He knows why He is waiting, even when I don't.

While I have unanswered questions, I look at Jesus, seeing what He was like, and I can rest with my unanswered questions. "A very good God has got this" is all I know in the depths of my soul. My prayer is that you would find that same kind of peace.

PRAYER

Father, thank You that I don't have to understand everything to trust You. Sometimes my heart aches with questions that seem to have no answers. But when I remember how Jesus suffered for us, I'm reminded that You're not distant from our pain. Help me rest in knowing that Your understanding is so much bigger than mine, even when nothing makes sense to me right now. Thank You for Jesus. In Jesus' name. Amen.

83

Finding Purpose in Your Pain

"Consider it pure joy, my brothers and sisters, whenever you face trials of many kinds, because you know that the testing of your faith produces perseverance." —James 1:2–3

If you made a list of your most painful experiences, and of times when you experienced the most growth or blessing, is it possible those two lists would have lots of crossover?

I can now understand how specific kinds of suffering that are in the service of growth can be a good thing. As a psychologist, I have often intentionally led people into deeper levels of pain in order for them to be healed. I can readily say "some pain is good for us." Facing painful feelings is curative when done well. I have admitted many people to hospitals as they screamed at me to let them go. I can feel for them in the process, but I do not hesitate at all in leading them into it. I know they will get better as a result.

So, some suffering we endure for good reasons, and I can also see what the Bible means when it says God can bring good out of even some of the worst things that happen to us. Things that He did not cause or lead us into. When He did not heal my hand in college and I lost my ability to play competitive golf, I could not understand it. I prayed, and nothing happened. But He was able to use that loss for my good and bring a greater healing.

Cancer is not good. But God can enter into that scenario and show His love and work in it to bring something good out of something so bad.

He may not heal it, for whatever unknown reason I still do not get, but we do know that God hurts when we suffer. He says it grieves Him when people suffer because of the abuse of others, the evil and selfishness of others, or other horrible realities. He empathizes with the sufferer and is relieved Himself when we enter in and relieve people's suffering.

PRAYER

Father, there's so much I don't understand about suffering, why some prayers for healing go unanswered, why good people face such hard times. But I'm grateful You're not distant from my pain—You're right here in it with me. Help me recognize the ways You might be using this season to shape me. Give me hope when healing feels far away, and eyes to see the good You're bringing from this challenge. In Jesus' name. Amen.

84

From Wounded to a Wounded Healer

Praise be to the God and Father of our Lord Jesus Christ, the Father of compassion and the God of all comfort, who comforts us in all our troubles, so that we can comfort those in any trouble with the comfort we ourselves have received from God.

—2 Corinthians 1:3–4

Has God ever used your pain to allow you to help someone else in a way no one else can?

There is no good answer to why there is suffering in the world other than the misused freedom given to man that turned evil. The Bible talks about an evil personal devil, Satan, who has an army who daily tempts people to do destructive things and causes suffering on earth. We sometimes open ourselves up to be used in his plot against God. We sometimes desire activities or devise plans that are not good for us. Mankind often offers themselves to be used by Satan to do evil without knowing they are being used.

The message of the Bible is clear: God hates suffering and evil so much that one day He will avenge it all and make it right. He will pour out His judgment on those who do evil and never repent. While God is in ultimate control, He is not the author of that suffering, and He certainly does not like it. He feels deeply for it and wants us to partner with Him to end it.

I do not know why He can allow it to go on. But there is some reason, which we cannot understand, why He can allow something He hates to continue for a while. For now, we can only trust Him, even as we don't understand.

Jesus said the devil is the one who "comes only to steal and kill and destroy; I have come that they may have life, and have it to the full" (John 10:10). We know Jesus did not cause suffering; He came to end it.

One last good thing about how suffering can be used for good: He can use our suffering to help others. How many times have you been helped by someone who is able to help you like no one else can, because they themself have been through what you are suffering with? The "wounded healer" is a reality.

Consider the struggles you've faced—how might God be preparing you to offer unique comfort to others facing similar challenges?

I admitted this is one of the toughest questions for me and it is still a great mystery. But I am okay now with waiting to know the final answer until the day I finally see Him. Until then, I believe "He's got this."

PRAYER

Father of all comfort, I need Your Presence today. When evil feels so real and pain cuts deep, remind me that You're not the author of my suffering—You're my helper through it. Thank You for walking with me in my darkest valleys. Give me strength to be a wounded healer, someone who can reach out to others because I know what it's like to hurt and find hope again. In Jesus' name. Amen.

85

When Your Faith and Career Seem to Clash

If any of you lacks wisdom, you should ask God, who gives generously to all without finding fault, and it will be given to you.

—James 1:5

Have you ever felt tension between your faith and your work, education, or other areas of your life?

I have been in the field of psychology for many decades now. It has been a long journey, and it is interesting to look back at that path and see how psychology proved the Bible to be true for me. Actually, surprisingly, it was the Bible that had to rescue me from the "psychology" I was learning from the church.

Many in the faith world saw secular psychology as being antithetical to faith, coming from a humanistic worldview having little to offer. There were models that taught that clinical issues all came from sin or not knowing enough Bible to order your thinking to wellness.

But as I gained more clinical experience, the Christian models began to fall short of both my scientific understanding and clinical experience. I saw them fall short . . . people were not getting well when they had had much treatment in those models of the "Christian way" of treating mental health issues.

I was learning that there were real clinical modalities and interventions and approaches to therapy that worked. I was seeing eating disorders healed, depression healed, anxiety states overcome, thought disorders "cured," trauma healed, and the like. I was falling in love with my field as I saw the fruits of clinical practice.

But in falling in love with all of that, I felt like I was an adulterer . . . my new love seemingly was not the love I was supposed to have with my faith and the Bible. I saw people getting well . . . but where was the faith as I understood it in all of this?

PRAYER

Lord, I struggle when different parts of my life seem to conflict with my faith. Thank You that You are the author of all truth—both in Your Word and in the world You created. Help me stay open to learning and growing, even when it challenges what I thought I knew. Guide me as I wrestle with these big questions. In Jesus' name. Amen.

86

What Happens When You Read the Bible with Fresh Eyes

The unfolding of your words gives light . . . Direct my footsteps according to your word. —Psalms 119:130, 133

When was the last time you approached Scripture without preconceptions, eager to discover what it actually says?

I *knew* God was real. And I *knew* that the Bible was true. But many of the Christian views I had learned of psychology were just not completely true, or, at the very least, the truth fell short. I knew too much to go back to thinking they were right or accepting them as they were being presented. I could not live with that, so I basically dropped out of life for the better part of a couple of years and spent every waking moment I could doing one thing: reading and studying my Bible. I was not going to read any of the Christian stuff about psychology or mental health issues. I already knew that literature. I wanted to see what the Bible said about these issues. And here is what happened:

I was "born-again, again."

I could not believe it. Literally everything I was learning in the science that showed where mental health, relational, and performance issues came from, as well as how to resolve them, was right there in the Scriptures. All along, it was all there.

My book *Changes That Heal* and those coauthored with John Townsend *Boundaries* and *How People Grow* came out of this work and this season.

What area of your life might benefit from setting aside what others have told you the Bible says and discovering for yourself what God's Word really teaches?

PRAYER

Father, when I feel stuck between what I've been taught and what I'm discovering, help me come to You directly. Open my eyes to see Your Word in new ways. Give me courage to look at Scripture with fresh eyes, even if it challenges what I think I know. Help me set aside time to really dig into Your Word. Thank You that Your truth is deep enough to keep teaching me new things. In Jesus' name. Amen.

87

God Taught It First

For the word of God is alive and active. Sharper than any double-edged sword, it penetrates even to dividing soul and spirit, joints and marrow; it judges the thoughts and attitudes of the heart.

—Hebrews 4:12

Have you ever been surprised to discover that a "modern insight" was actually an ancient biblical principle?

I recall a conversation with a woman on an airplane. Usually, I avoid saying I'm a psychologist, as I know what's coming—a long session when I'd rather watch Netflix. But that day, I let it slip.

"Oh my gosh," she said. "I have to tell you about my boyfriend. I just broke up with him again and I am heart-broken. We break up because I can't live with it, then I miss him, take him back because I love him. It's good for a minute, then it happens again."

"What happens that's so painful?" I asked.

"His anger. He gets so angry, and it's hurtful, and I get scared. Whenever I don't do what he wants, he gets angry. He tries to control me and he rages."

"What makes it better?"

"I know how to calm him down. I just do whatever he wants, and then he's fine. We have peace . . . but I can't always do that. I feel like I'm losing myself. So we break up and then I go back."

"Well," I said. "There's an old saying: 'If you rescue an angry man, you will only have to do it again.' Keep going back and rescuing him from his anger by complying, and you'll calm him down, but it will only repeat itself."

"That's amazing! Where did you get that?"

"The Bible," I said. "Proverbs 19:19."

"Wait . . . that's in the Bible?"

"Yep. Go check it out."

I found she was like many others—we often don't know what the Bible says about these issues. For instance, issues that have become popular in addiction science lately have been taught in the Bible for centuries. I'd been in church for years, yet never learned about "boundaries" there. I learned that from psychology. Then, when I went back to the Bible, there it was all along.

It's yet another thing that further validated my faith, another pillar of "why I believe."

What challenges are you facing right now where God's Word might offer wisdom you've overlooked or never been taught?

PRAYER

God, sometimes I forget just how much wisdom You packed into Your Word. Thank You for loving us enough to give us practical guidance for our relationships and daily struggles. Help me dive deeper into Scripture, expecting to find real answers. When I face tough situations with others, remind me to look first to Your Word for wisdom. Give me the courage to apply what You teach me, even when it's hard. In Jesus' name. Amen.

88

When God Invades Your Closed System

"Abide in Me, and I in you. As the branch cannot bear fruit of itself, unless it abides in the vine, neither can you, unless you abide in Me." —John 15:4 NKJV

Where in your life do you feel stuck in patterns that seem to be getting worse rather than better?

I remember where I was as a graduate student, on the sixth tee at one of my favorite golf courses, when a thought hit me. Psychology began with Freud, who came from physics and biology, which taught about hydraulics. "Push down here and the water shoots out from over there." Repress an emotion, and it squirts out as a symptom somewhere else.

Thermodynamics! A closed system gets worse over time, and the only way to reverse that is to open the system and infuse the two ingredients of energy and intelligence from the outside to make the energy useful. That is psychological development and healing in a nutshell!

The human psyche can be a closed system. And it gets worse if it remains closed. But if it opens up to two outside ingredients, new energy and new intelligence to utilize that energy, as physics teaches, the psyche grows.

Consider the areas where you've been trying to grow or heal on your own—how might inviting God's energy and wisdom into those closed systems create a breakthrough?

All the psychological research ever done in meta-analyses of therapies has one finding over all others: it is the therapeutic relationship that heals. And that relationship has to be a supportive energy with warmth (love) and intelligence (truth and guiding principles, wisdom, knowledge, insight, and structure).

In terms of my faith, it explained the whole message of the Bible:

1. We were created to be connected to energy (God) and intelligence (God).
2. We separated from Him and became individual "closed systems" without the energy from the relationship with God and His love, and without His "ways" living in us.
3. Entropy had its way and humanity got worse as we remained separated from Love and helpful input of Intelligence beyond ourselves.

4. Then, God entered the system, human life, Himself to bring us back to connection with Him.

That is the gospel in a nutshell.

When I reconnected to Him, I found a Source of energy and love and support that I needed, and His ways healed me and set me on a different path of growth. He invaded my "closed system."

PRAYER

Lord, sometimes I feel like a closed system—stuck, stagnant, and running on empty. Thank You for showing me that You're always ready to pour Your energy and wisdom into my life. Help me to stay open to You, to receive Your love fully, and to let Your truth guide me. Give me the courage to break down the walls I've built and truly connect with You. I want to abide in Jesus. In Jesus' name. Amen.

89

Entering into the Relationship You Were Made For

"Behold, I stand at the door and knock. If anyone hears My voice and opens the door, I will come in to him and dine with him, and he with Me." —Revelation 3:20 NKJV

Perhaps you opened this book with little faith—or faith that felt fragile. Maybe a friend who saw your struggles encouraged you to read it. But now, as we reach these final pages, something has shifted. Some of your questions have found answers. You've caught glimpses of a God who is alive and at work. You've taken steps toward belief. Now you're ready for the next one.

I want to invite you to take that next step. For some, it might feel like your very first step of faith. For others, it may be the same step I took that day in my college dorm room, which took my faith to a deeper level. Or it could be a reboot of faith, as your path has taken you in some different directions.

Whatever your story, could it be that your deepest longing for connection is actually a longing for God.

Faith in Jesus is not primarily a collection of "beliefs" or a philosophy. It is a *relationship*. It is the relationship that God created you for in the very beginning of why He made you. He created you to love you, and share love, life, and purpose with you. In fact, as I have told many, you can begin by just sincerely asking Him, "Are You real? If so, show me. I am open to knowing."

The Bible reveals that each of us have breached that relationship in various ways. We either have ignored, rejected, or strayed away from Him.

But He wants us! He wants us back in the relationship that was lost with Him. Just like when you have been betrayed in one of your personal relationships, reconciling takes forgiveness. The one who betrayed you has to do something simple: own what they did and ask for your forgiveness. Then, when you forgive them, the two of you can start anew.

This is the message of the Gospel of Jesus. He comes to us, invites us to just admit we have turned against God and failed His perfect standard in various ways, and simply receive the forgiveness He is offering, thereby having our relationship reconciled.

The "good news" is that we get a clean slate. No judgment or condemnation awaits. We have all sinned in some way. But the good news is that the Judge Himself says He will pay our fine for us. That is what the death of Christ was about. He "paid" for our sins that deserve judgment. When we accept Him, we are forgiven.

———PRAYER———

Father, I've wandered pretty far, trying to do life on my own terms. But I'm tired of keeping You at arm's length. Today, I hear You knocking, and I want to open that door. Thank you for never giving up on me, for offering me a clean slate despite my mistakes. I accept Your invitation to start fresh and begin to follow You. Help me learn what it means to walk with Jesus daily. In Jesus' name. Amen.

90

Your Invitation

That is, the message concerning faith that we proclaim: If you declare with your mouth, "Jesus is Lord," and believe in your heart that God raised him from the dead, you will be saved. For it is with your heart that you believe and are justified, and it is with your mouth that you profess your faith and are saved.

—Romans 10:8–10

While many readers of this book are believers seeking to deepen their faith, I know others have been reading from a different perspective. Perhaps you've been exploring Christianity from the outside looking in, wondering if there's something real here that you've been missing. Maybe you've been carrying questions that, until now, no one has been able to answer. Or possibly you've been watching a friend or family member live out their faith and wondering what drives them.

If any of that sounds like you, I want you to know: these final words are especially for you. The door is wide open. God is waiting with open arms.

So, can I gently ask: What's holding you back from taking God's hand and stepping into the life He's offering you?

Yesterday I started telling you about the invitation you have from God, to receive His forgiveness through Jesus and enter into a relationship with Him. Today—our final day—I want to continue with that invitation.

I mentioned you need to receive God's forgiveness. The first step—as it would be in any relationship—is to tell Him you are sorry for sinning against Him.

That second step is called repentance, which basically means to do an about face, to change direction. Instead of being the god of our lives, we decide that He will be our Lord. We agree to answer to Him.

It sounds simple and hard to believe, but it really is a free gift. You don't have to be good enough. You just need to say yes to receiving His forgiveness.

And there is more good news . . . He knows we won't do it perfectly in the future. We will make mistakes along the way. He promises to continue to forgive and, past that, to help us grow and get better. As the Bible says, His mercies "are new every morning" (Lam. 3:23). Just like a good parent, He will be with you as you learn and grow, and help you continue to turn into the best person you were designed to be.

He also doesn't want you to do this alone. He says that once you come "home" to being back with your Heavenly Father, you will need some good "brothers and sisters" to live it all out with, in relationship together. So, find a good group of people (a church) who are on that path with you, and who can help you. (Don't let that word "church" scare you . . . there really are some good ones out there. ☺)

And I would strongly suggest beginning by reading the gospel of John. In John, you'll read about the life of Jesus and get to know Him better.

In John, Jesus made a claim no one else makes. He said, "I am the way and the truth and the life. No one comes to the Father except through me" (John 14:6). Some see it as exclusive, but He invites *everyone*—so it is *not* exclusive at all.

So, as we close, I would like to pass on to you that invitation. He promised that if anyone seeks Him with their whole heart, they will find Him. Open the door, and watch. He will begin to reveal Himself if you truly want to know Him. Imagine your life might look like if you took this step of faith—how might your perspective, your purpose, and your relationships be transformed.

PRAYER

God, I'm here, and I want to be honest with You. Sometimes it feels overwhelming to make such a big change, but I know You're waiting with open arms. Help me understand what it means to make You Lord of my life. Thank You for promising to walk with me every step of the way, even when I stumble. Show me what it looks like to truly follow Jesus. In Jesus' name. Amen.

About the Author

DR. HENRY CLOUD is an acclaimed leadership expert, clinical psychologist, and *New York Times* bestselling author. His forty-six books, including the iconic *Boundaries*, have sold nearly twenty million copies worldwide. He has an extensive executive coaching background and experience as a leadership consultant, devoting the majority of his time to working with CEOs, leadership teams, and executives to improve performance, leadership skills, and culture.

Additional Copyright Information